THE USBORNE BOOK OF
EXPLORERS

Felicity Everett
and Struan Reid
History consultant: Anne Millard

Designed by Russell Punter

Illustrated by Peter Dennis

Additional illustrations by Richard Draper,
Peter Goodwin & Ian Jackson

Series editor: Anthony Marks

With thanks to Philip Roxbee Cox

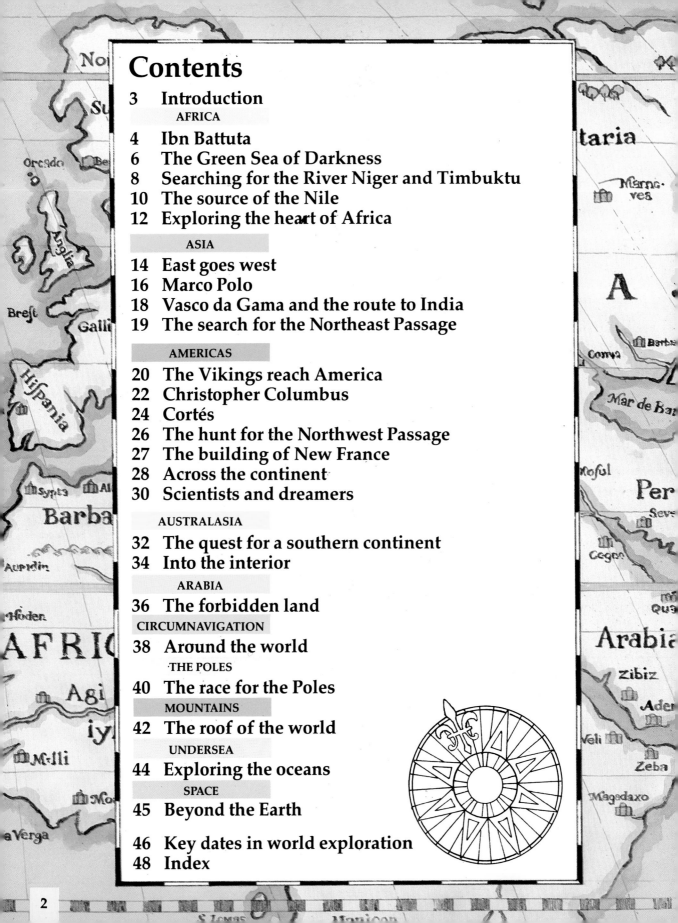

Contents

Introduction

This book tells the stories of the lives of some of the world's greatest explorers. It is not a comprehensive history of exploration, but it describes in detail the voyages of discovery that have had the most impact on the world.

What is an explorer?

Many of the explorers in this book were not the first people to set foot in the lands they visited, as the local inhabitants had been there for thousands of years. But they are thought of as explorers because they all changed the way people thought about the world. For example, Europeans returned from the Far East or America with important geographical information. Darwin's findings on the Galapagos Islands led him to challenge our basic ideas about the evolution of the planet.

Exploration is a way of learning about the world. As early travellers went further afield, they unravelled the mysteries of unknown continents. And even today, there are aspects of the Earth, and of space, that are still not fully understood. Each time scientists probe the frontiers of space, and when divers examine the sea bed, they continue to expand our knowledge with their explorations.

Why people explore

Throughout history, people have had an insatiable appetite for knowledge and adventure. But there have also been more specific reasons for exploration.

The competition for food forced our earliest ancestors in all directions in search of new places to live. Huge and powerful empires were built up through trade and

Mosaic of a Roman merchant ship.

conquest by the early civilizations - the Minoans, the Egyptians, the Phoenicians, the Greeks and the Romans.

Religion has always played an important part in the exploration of new lands. As early as the 5th century, Irish monks set out to convert the people of Wales, Cornwall and France to Christianity. But some later expeditions, though carried out

A 6th-century stone cross.

in the name of religion, were in fact accompanied by appalling savagery and destruction.

There were amateur explorers with a desire to see new places, like Ibn Battuta, Hsuan-tsang and Richard Burton. Others, such as Alexander Humboldt and Charles Darwin, led scientific expeditions which set out to learn as much as possible about the new lands.

How we know about exploration

Explorers, whether on land or on sea, have always kept records of the new lands and peoples they encountered, and some have used these to write books. The Greek explorer Diogenes' account of his journey inland from the east coast of Africa in the 1st century AD helped Ptolemy to draw his map of the world in the next century. In the 14th century, Ibn Battuta wrote down all he saw on his travels. Europeans

Medieval map

soon developed a taste for the accounts of mystery and adventure. Mungo Park wrote a book about his travels in Africa which was a best-seller, and Stanley's latest reports from Africa were eagerly awaited.

Geographical arrangement

The book is arranged into groups, according to region: Africa, Asia, the Americas, and Australasia. There are also individual pages on Arabia, the Poles, Circumnavigation, Mountains, Undersea and Space.

Each section is introduced with a small map showing the areas covered, and a chart giving the most important dates in the exploration of that region. There is also a more detailed date chart on pages 46-47 that shows all the events in the book in one list.

Dates

Many of the dates are from the period before the birth of Christ. They are indicated by the letters BC. Early dates in the period after Christ's birth are indicated by the letters AD. Some of the dates begin with the abbreviation "c". This stands for *circa*, the Latin for "about" and is used when historians are unsure exactly when an event took place.

Maps

There are detailed maps on many pages. These show the routes taken by the explorers, and also many of the places they visited.

Ibn Battuta

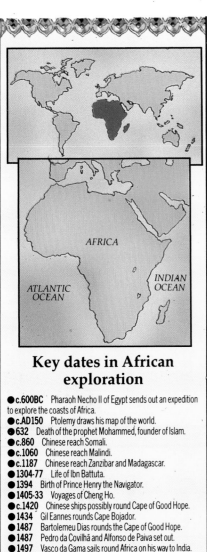

Key dates in African exploration

- **c.600BC** Pharaoh Necho II of Egypt sends out an expedition to explore the coasts of Africa.
- **c.AD150** Ptolemy draws his map of the world.
- **632** Death of the prophet Mohammed, founder of Islam.
- **c.860** Chinese reach Somali.
- **c.1060** Chinese reach Malindi.
- **c.1187** Chinese reach Zanzibar and Madagascar.
- **1304-77** Life of Ibn Battuta.
- **1394** Birth of Prince Henry the Navigator.
- **1405-33** Voyages of Cheng Ho.
- **c.1420** Chinese ships possibly round Cape of Good Hope.
- **1434** Gil Eannes rounds Cape Bojador.
- **1487** Bartolemeu Dias rounds the Cape of Good Hope.
- **1487** Pedro da Covilhã and Alfonso de Paiva set out.
- **1497** Vasco da Gama sails round Africa on his way to India.
- **1795** Mungo Park sails to Africa.
- **1805** Park leaves on his second trip to Africa.
- **1824** René Caillié sets out from France for Timbuktu.
- **1851** David Livingstone, his family and Cotton Oswell cross the Kalahari Desert.
- **1852-56** Livingstone becomes the first European to walk right across Africa.
- **1856** Richard Burton and John Speke leave England in search of the source of the Nile.
- **1858** Speke claims to have discovered the source of the Nile.
- **1858** Livingstone sets out to explore Zambezi River.
- **1860** Speke and James Grant leave on second journey to Africa.
- **1871** Henry Stanley and Livingstone meet at Ujiji.
- **1872** Livingstone starts out on his last journey, round the southern shores of Lake Tanganyika.
- **1874** Stanley returns to Africa to map lakes Victoria and Tanganyika.
- **1876-77** Stanley sails down the Lualaba and Congo rivers to the Atlantic.
- **1887** Stanley goes in search of Emin Pasha in the Sudan.

In the seventh century AD, the prophet Mohammed founded a new religion called Islam in Mecca, Arabia. Within a century of his death in 632 his followers, known as Muslims, had conquered a huge empire in the Middle East and North Africa.

Ibn Battuta was a rich Moroccan Muslim who in 1325 set out on a pilgrimage to Mecca. His adventures inspired him to travel further. He made daring journeys through parts of Africa, the Middle East and the Far East that before then were largely unknown to Europeans.

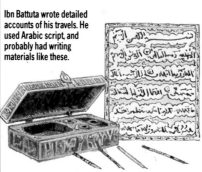

Ibn Battuta wrote detailed accounts of his travels. He used Arabic script, and probably had writing materials like these.

Through the Middle East

Ibn Battuta crossed Egypt to the Red Sea, hoping to sail to Jeddah. Because of a tribal war, however, he had to abandon his plans and go back to Cairo. He travelled on to Jerusalem and Damascus, then made his way by land through Arabia to Mecca.

From Mecca he travelled north to Baghdad, and was horrified that the city had been destroyed by the Mongols (fierce Asian warriors). He visited Anatolia (now part of Turkey), then went back to Mecca where he studied law. His new profession enabled him to pay for more travelling, and he soon set off again.

Around the coast of Africa

Ibn Battuta next crossed the Red Sea to Aden. There he boarded a dhow (a type of ship) which was heading for Zaila in Somalia. In his journal, he described Zaila as the dirtiest place he had ever visited.

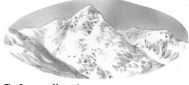

Dhows are still quite common on the coast of East Africa.

From Zaila Ibn Battuta sailed on down the coast to Mombasa and Kilwa. He was impressed by the fine wooden houses there, and intrigued by the dark skins of the Africans.

Further afield

To get back to Mecca Ibn Battuta sailed along the south coast of Arabia and into the Persian Gulf, then crossed the Arabian Peninsula. Before long, however, his curiosity made him impatient to travel again.

The Caucasus Mountains

This time he headed north to Syria, Kaffa (the Crimea), and the Caucasus Mountains. He later crossed Central Asia, through Afghanistan, to India. From India he travelled by sea to Canton in China, then began the return journey to Morocco (via Malaysia and India). He eventually reached Fez in 1349.

A caravan crossing the Sahara desert

Timbuktu as it might have looked in Ibn Battuta's time.

Across the Sahara

In 1352 Ibn Battuta set out again, this time to explore Africa. In many ways this was his most important expedition, for he was able to write about parts of the world that were unrecorded by other travellers at that time.

He crossed the Sahara Desert, heading for Mali. Conditions were harsh and bandits roamed the desert, so for protection he joined a caravan (a procession of traders and other travellers who used camels for transport).

First the caravan stopped in Taghaza, where Ibn Battuta noted that all the buildings were made of salt and camel skins. The travellers picked up supplies of water for the next ten days' journey to Tasarahla.

Then came the trek to Walata, which was made very dangerous because of shifting sands. Progress was slow, and there was the risk the water would run out.

Into unknown territory

Despite these dangers Ibn Battuta crossed the Sahara safely. He reached Mali, then continued as far as the River Niger. This was very daring, as few travellers had ventured that far into the African interior before. The territory was so forbidding (see pages 8-13) that it was not further explored for another 400 years.

For the return journey, he chose an equally challenging route. This time he visited Timbuktu, an ancient city famed for its wealth and splendour.

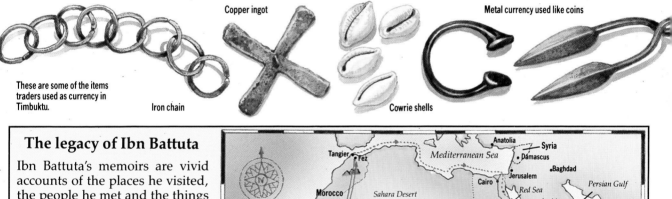

Copper ingot

Metal currency used like coins

These are some of the items traders used as currency in Timbuktu.

Iron chain

Cowrie shells

The legacy of Ibn Battuta

Ibn Battuta's memoirs are vivid accounts of the places he visited, the people he met and the things he saw. Many people did not believe the strange stories he brought back from his travels.

This map shows the routes of Ibn Battuta's journeys in Africa. These, combined with his travels in Asia and the Far East, covered an amazing 120,700km (75,000 miles). This is more than many of today's travellers manage, even with all the benefits of modern methods of transport.

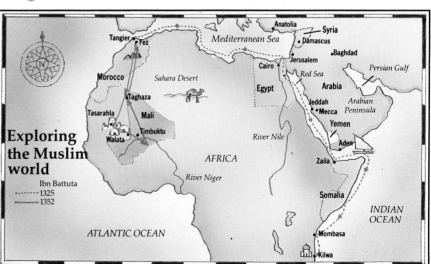

Exploring the Muslim world

Ibn Battuta
...... 1325
— 1352

Tangier • Fez
Morocco
Taghaza
Tasarahla
Mali
Walata
Timbuktu

Sahara Desert

AFRICA

River Niger

ATLANTIC OCEAN

Mediterranean Sea
Anatolia
Syria
Damascus
Baghdad
Jerusalem
Cairo
Red Sea
Persian Gulf
Egypt
Arabia
Jeddah
Mecca
Arabian Peninsula
Yemen
River Nile
Aden
Zaila
Somalia
INDIAN OCEAN
Mombasa
Kilwa

The Green Sea of Darkness

The first known journey round Africa took place about 600BC. Pharaoh Necho II of Egypt sent a sea captain to explore the coasts of Africa. The voyage was not repeated for almost two thousand years.

An Egyptian boat on a trading mission.

Europeans became interested in Africa during the Middle Ages. They acquired a taste for luxuries from the East such as spices, silks, sugar, pearls and precious stones. But the overland trade routes to the East were controlled by the Turks, who were at war with the Europeans. This made these goods very rare and expensive and the Europeans wanted to obtain them more cheaply. They became determined to find a sea route round Africa, avoiding the Turks, so that they could trade directly with India, China and the Spice Islands (now the Moluccas) in the Pacific Ocean.

The explorer who stayed at home

Prince Henry of Portugal was born in 1394 and later devoted his life to discovery. He was lured by the riches of the East and inspired by the stories of the Christian priest-king known as Prester John who was believed to live somewhere in Africa.

Henry the Navigator (1394-1460) Although the area opened up by his sailors was comparatively small, they took the first and most difficult steps into unknown lands.

In 1419 Henry was appointed Governor of the Algarve, in southern Portugal. On the wind-swept, rocky coast at Sagres, near the most southwesterly point of Europe (called by Europeans "the end of the world"), he built a palace, a church, a school to train navigators and pilots, an observatory and a shipyard. He recruited scholars, geographers, astronomers and mariners. He bullied and inspired his courtiers to lead expeditions that would open up new trade routes.

A barrier of fear

Henry sent out 14 expeditions over 12 years, but each one turned back at Cape Bojador on the west coast of Africa near the Canary Islands. This was as far south as the sailors dared go. They believed that at the Equator, in an area known as the "Green Sea of Darkness", the sun was so close to the Earth that people's skins were burned black, the sea boiled and there were whirlpools and thick green fogs where monsters lurked waiting to devour them.

The great breakthrough

Then, in 1434, one of Henry's courtiers called Gil Eannes managed to persuade his crew to carry on beyond the dreaded Cape. They survived to tell the tale, and from then on other Portuguese expeditions ventured further and further south.

None of Henry's ships had managed to sail round the southern tip of Africa by the time he died in 1460. But his inspiration paved the way for the journeys that would open up the world. Although he himself never sailed on any of the voyages he planned, he is always known as Henry the Navigator.

St Mary's rose, picked by Eannes from beyond Bojador.

This Portuguese ship was called a caravel. It was very sturdy and could travel long distances.

Round the Cape

In August 1487 King John II of Portugal sent out an expedition of three ships from Lisbon. It was led by Bartolemeu Dias, who was instructed to open the sea route round Africa's southern tip. King John believed that the way east would be clear once the Indian Ocean was reached.

John II
(reigned 1481-95)

Off Cape Volta the ships were caught in a terrible storm which lasted nearly two weeks. The terrified sailors were blown round the southern tip of Africa and into the Indian Ocean. They sailed north to the Great Fish River and then turned round for home.

On their way back to Portugal, Dias and his crew saw the Cape and realized their achievement.

A Portuguese ship rounding the Cape of Good Hope.

Dias named it "Cabo Tormentoso", the Cape of Storms. King John renamed it the Cape of Good Hope, for a sea route to the East had been found.

Two spies set out

Pedro da Covilhã was one of the King of Portugal's courtiers and an experienced spy. In May 1487, he and Alfonso de Paiva set out on a secret mission. Covilhã was to find out all he could about the route to India, while Paiva was to seek out Prester John's kingdom in Africa. First they travelled to Rhodes where they disguised themselves as Arab traders and joined a party of merchants travelling to Egypt. They sailed to Cairo where they boarded a boat travelling down the Red Sea to Suakin in the Sudan. Here they parted company.

Paiva set off in search of Prester John, while Covilhã sailed for southwest India. He noted every detail of his voyages, of the geography along the way, and of the fabulous cargoes of cinnamon, cloves, pepper, silks, rugs and precious stones. At Goa, superb Arab horses were sold to the Indian rulers.

A new adventure

From India Covilhã sailed to the Persian Gulf, then on down the east coast of Africa. Returning to Cairo in 1490 he learned that Paiva had died without finding Prester John. Covilhã himself took up the search for the elusive monarch, whose kingdom was by this time thought to be Abyssinia (now Ethiopia). He sent a report of his travels to the King of Portugal, then set off south. First of all he visited the holy city of Mecca (see page 4) dressed as a Muslim pilgrim.

The happy captive

Although Abyssinia was a Christian country, Covilhã was surprised and disappointed to find that it was not the fabulously rich kingdom he expected. (Prester John was never found, but stories of his empire persisted well into the 16th century.)

Perhaps because he had seen too much, Covilhã was forbidden to leave Abyssinia and spent the remaining 30 years of his life there. He was treated well in his new homeland, eventually marrying a rich local woman. From time to time he entertained ambassadors from Europe and he encouraged trade between Abyssinia and Portugal.

This is how 15th-century Europeans imagined Prester John.

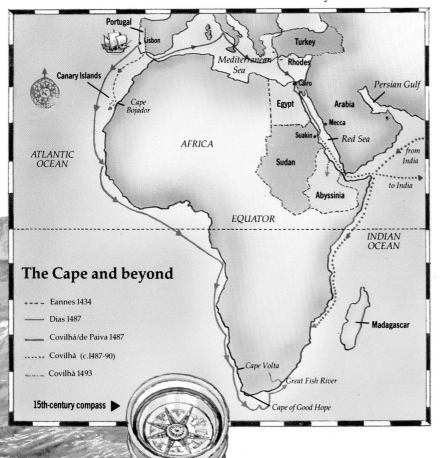

The Cape and beyond

---- Eannes 1434
—— Dias 1487
—— Covilhã/de Paiva 1487
..... Covilhã (c.1487-90)
~~~ Covilhã 1493

15th-century compass ▶

Portugal
Lisbon
Turkey
Mediterranean Sea
Rhodes
Canary Islands
Cairo
Egypt
Arabia
Persian Gulf
Cape Bojador
Mecca
Suakin
Red Sea
ATLANTIC OCEAN
AFRICA
Sudan
from India
to India
Abyssinia
EQUATOR
INDIAN OCEAN
Madagascar
Cape Volta
Great Fish River
Cape of Good Hope

Searching for the River Niger and Timbuktu

The Romans were the first Europeans to explore the interior of Africa. After their conquest of Egypt and the north African coast during the 1st century BC, they sent various expeditions over the Atlas Mountains and into the Sahara Desert, usually in pursuit of nomadic tribes who had attacked their soldiers and then disappeared.

Scientific explorers

Europeans set up trading stations along the coastline of Africa from the 15th century, but the traders ventured only a little way inland. During the 18th century, however, a new spirit of scientific enquiry grew up. In 1788 the Association for Promoting the Discovery of the Interior Parts of Africa was founded. It aimed to find and plot the course of the mysterious River Niger and to find the legendary trading city of Timbuktu, famed for its riches and palaces. But the first expeditions were failures, with the explorers dying from terrible diseases and heat.

The adventurous doctor

In 1794 a young Scottish doctor called Mungo Park was chosen to lead an expedition to the source of the River Niger to find out whether it flowed into the sea or into a lake. Park left England by ship in May 1795, and arrived at Pisania in the Gambia two months later. He stayed there for some months studying the local language and eventually set off into the African interior in December.

Mungo Park (1771-1806)

Park would have carried a sextant similar to this, to calculate distances.

The Niger is sighted

At first all went well and Park was hospitably received. However, things started to go wrong when his guides became frightened and refused to go any further. Some of the local rulers robbed him of all his possessions until he had nothing left except the clothes he wore and his horse. Finally he was captured by horsemen and held prisoner.

Park was attacked and stripped of all his belongings.

Park was kept in terrible conditions in an isolated hut on the edge of the desert for four months. Late one night in June 1796 he managed to escape from his prison. But instead of heading back to the coast and safety he pressed on with his mission, travelling through the thick forests to avoid being seen. A month later he reached Segu and caught his first glimpse of the Niger. He was overjoyed and was able to confirm once and for all that the river flowed eastwards.

Park had managed to save the notes he had made throughout his adventures by carefully hiding them. After his return to Scotland, he used the notes to write a book called *Travels in the Interior Districts of Africa*. It quickly became a best-seller. But the lure of Africa proved too great and Park was eager to return and explore it further.

An illustration from Park's book, showing him knocking at the gates of a village to escape from a lion.

A doomed expedition

In January 1805 Park set sail for Pisania once more, this time to travel the whole length of the Niger. He went with a larger expedition of 30 soldiers and ten other Europeans. The expedition was doomed from the start. Park was impatient to leave, even though it was the rainy season. By the time they reached the Niger the river was swollen and 29 members of the team had died of exhaustion and disease.

Park was determined to carry on, for the river turned south towards the Atlantic. At Sansanding he found two old canoes and joined them together, intending to float down the Niger to the sea. But by now the party was reduced to just nine members. This exhausted group reached the rapids at Boussa, 805km (500 miles) from the mouth of the river. Here they were attacked by warriors of the local king. Park and his men drowned when their boat capsized.

Park and his team being attacked by African warriors.

Inspired by travel stories

At the beginning of the 1820's, the Geographical Society of Paris offered a prize of 10,000 francs to the first Frenchman to reach the city of Timbuktu and return. René Caillié, a young man from a poor family, heard of the competition and was determined to win the prize. He had wanted to become an explorer since reading *Robinson Crusoe* by Daniel Defoe. He began careful preparations for the journey and plotted his route. He worked hard and saved enough money to pay for everything himself, including equipment and helpers. In 1824 Caillié left France and sailed to Senegal on the west coast of Africa and remained there for three years, learning the Arabic language and finding out about the Muslim faith.

In April 1827 Caillié and his team of ten Africans joined a caravan and set off for the Rio Nuñez between Sierra Leone and Senegal. In June they reached Kouroussa on the Niger. They set off on the next leg of the journey, but soon afterwards Caillié fell ill with malaria and scurvy. Five months

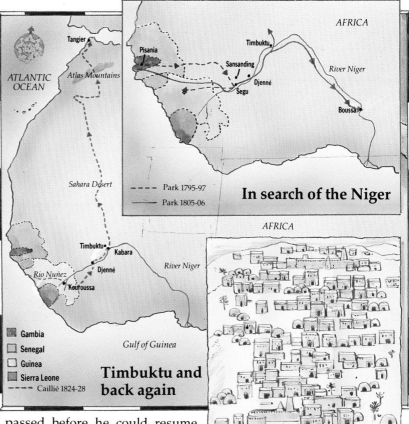

In search of the Niger

Timbuktu and back again

René Caillié (1799-1838)

Caillié in Arabic dress.

Caillié travelling through the African jungle.

passed before he could resume the journey. It was not until March 1828 that the little party reached Djenné, having walked nearly the entire distance of 1,610km (1,000 miles). From there they were able to sail down the Niger another 805km (500 miles) to Kabara, the port near Timbuktu.

Excitement and disappointment

They finally reached Timbuktu in April. For Caillié this moment, which he had looked forward to for years, was an anticlimax. The fabled city looked poor, neglected and drab. The trade in gold from Guinea had ceased many years before and the great trade caravans no longer visited it.

Caillié's sketch of Timbuktu. The city was a pale shadow of the rich place it had once been.

However, Caillié was welcomed by the inhabitants and stayed for two weeks. Then he joined a 1,000-strong camel caravan taking slaves and other goods across the Sahara. This return journey was hard and long, and he experienced such thirst that he could think only of water. When he reached Tangier, the officials there could not believe someone of his humble background could have travelled to Timbuktu and back. It was not until he was back in France that a panel of judges awarded him the prize.

9

The source of the Nile

The valley of the River Nile in Egypt is one of the most fertile areas in the world. Crops have been grown there since ancient times and the river has been a source of life to millions of people, many of whom have worshipped it as a god. But the origin of its waters remained a mystery for thousands of years. In the 5th century BC the Greek historian Herodotus wrote: "Of the sources of the Nile no-one can give any account." He believed that the river began at a fountain at the foot of some high mountains.

Over the centuries many expeditions tried to follow the river from Egypt to its source. One of the first of these was led by two Roman soldiers sent out by the Emperor Nero. But they had to abandon their journey when they reached a huge, impenetrable swamp known today as the Sudd. Later expeditions were defeated by the great distance, perilous swamps and stifling heat. In addition many explorers caught dreadful fevers.

In about AD150 a Greek geographer called Ptolemy drew a map of the world from various pieces of information. On it he showed two great lakes in Africa near a range of snow-capped mountains he called the Mountains of the Moon. He claimed that these lakes were the source of the Nile.

The Nile

Ptolemy's map

The rivals

By the middle of the 19th century no more was known about the source than in Ptolemy's days. In the 1840s German missionaries reported seeing two mountains, their tops covered with snow.

Richard Burton (1821-90)

John Speke (1827-64)

These were Mount Kilimanjaro and Mount Kenya. They also heard of the existence of two great lakes lying further inland. They were sure that these were the mountains and lakes on Ptolemy's map.

Many explorers and geographers wanted to be first to solve the mystery. In 1856 the Royal Geographical Society of London appointed Richard Burton as leader of a new expedition, with John Speke as his deputy. They had travelled together before but they made an unusual pair. Burton was a flamboyant and brilliant scholar who spoke 29 languages and had written numerous books; Speke was a quiet and careful planner. But both men were ruthless and determined.

A view of the port at Zanzibar.

They sailed to Zanzibar, an important slave market off the east coast of Africa where they recruited the rest of their team. In June 1857 the expedition – consisting of about 130 porters, 30 donkeys and enough provisions to last two years – set off for the Sea of Ujiji (now called Lake Tanganyika). They believed this was one of Ptolemy's lakes and that it would prove to be the source of the Nile.

But after only two weeks both Burton and Speke were suffering from malaria. It took the expedition five months to make its way to Tabora, a large slave market lying between Zanzibar and the Sea of Ujiji. The two men were exhausted and had to rest for a month. Shortly after setting off again, however, they both became extremely ill. Burton's legs became paralyzed and Speke went deaf and blind. It was some time before they both recovered.

The expedition sets out for the Sea of Ujiji in 1857.

Some of the equipment carried by Speke and Burton.

Discovery and disappointment

Eventually, on 13 February 1858, they reached the Sea of Ujiji and spent three and a half months

Part of the team exploring the Sea of Ujiji.

exploring the area. But their hopes were dashed when they questioned some local people and discovered that although there was a great river at the northern end, it flowed into the lake, not out of it. This indicated that it came from elsewhere and was not the Nile.

Although the discovery of the lake was important, Burton and Speke were very disappointed that they had not found the source of the Nile and they returned to Tabora. Burton was pleased to be among the Arab slave dealers again as he had travelled in Arabia (see page 37) and spoke Arabic. But Speke knew little Arabic and felt excluded. As he was impatient to leave, the two men parted. Burton stayed to rest while Speke left to try and locate another great lake to the north, Lake N'yanza, which he had heard about but which no European had yet seen.

The start of a feud

After an easy journey of just 16 days, Speke reached Mwanza on the southern shores of the lake. The pale blue waters stretched out endlessly before him. He was certain that he had at last found the

Speke on the shores of Lake N'yanza (Lake Victoria).

source of the Nile. But he did not explore it thoroughly enough to prove his theory. He renamed his discovery Lake Victoria after Britain's queen, then hurried back to Burton to tell him the news. Burton is believed to have been furious. He may have been jealous of Speke's discovery, or angry that his partner had relied on guesswork and not collected enough evidence to back up his claim.

The two men decided to return to England and travelled as far as Zanzibar. Burton became too sick to continue. He and Speke parted, agreeing not to break the news of their discoveries until both were back home. Speke, however, rushed back, and by the time Burton returned he had already reported the expedition's findings and taken most of the credit for them. A bitter feud then broke out between the two men when Speke, rather than Burton, was appointed to lead a new expedition to Lake Victoria.

The second expedition

Speke and his second-in-command, James Grant, left for Africa in the spring of 1860. It was not until the end of 1861 that they reached the unknown territory of Karagwe at the southern end of Lake Victoria. In January 1862 they became the first Europeans to enter Uganda,

James Grant (1827-92)

Ugandan tribespeople entertain Speke and Grant.

where they met the young King Mutesa. They remained there until July, when they moved on. Grant soon fell seriously ill but, rather than wait for him to recover, Speke travelled on alone. On 21 July 1862 he arrived at Urondogani, where he stood alone on the banks of a river flowing north out of Lake Victoria. He was now certain that he was looking at the beginnings of the Nile and that Lake Victoria was the source. But once again he failed to explore thoroughly enough to prove beyond doubt that the river became the Nile.

A mysterious death

Speke and Grant returned triumphant to England, but there was still uncertainty about Speke's findings. To settle the dispute, a final public discussion with Burton was arranged, to take place before a panel of scholars. But in September 1864, the day before the meeting was due to take place, Speke died in a shooting accident. There were rumours of suicide – perhaps he did not dare to face the brilliant Burton. It was many years before Lake Victoria was finally proved to be the main source of the Nile by the explorer and journalist H.M. Stanley (see page 13).

Memorial to Speke in Kensington Gardens, London.

IN MEMORY OF
SPEKE
VICTORIA NYANZA
AND THE NILE
1864

11

Exploring the heart of Africa

A line of Africans being marched away to be sold into slavery.

D avid Livingstone came from a very poor Scottish family, and at the age of ten went to work in a cotton mill. However he was determined to study, and while he was working in the mill he also taught himself Greek, Latin and mathematics. This enabled him to go to Glasgow University. At the age of 25 he qualified as a doctor and in 1840 he was ordained a Christian missionary and sent to Cape Town in South Africa to do religious and social work.

In 1843 Livingstone founded his own mission at Kolobeng, south of the Kalahari Desert. Apart from his religious work, he was also fired by the idea of the eradication of slavery. Throughout his travels in Africa he was to be constantly reminded of this cruel trade in human life. He set about opening up the unknown central regions of Africa, so other Christian missionaries and Europeans could follow. He believed that this would lead to the collapse of the slave trade.

David Livingstone (1813-73)

◀ The Victoria Falls

Livingstone's travels

His first success in exploration, after two earlier failures, was to cross the wilderness of the Kalahari Desert in 1851 and reach Lake Ngami on the northern edge of the desert. His wife Mary and their children also accompanied him, as well as his great friend Cotton Oswell. They all nearly died when their guide lost his way and they ran out of food and water. In 1852 Livingstone's family returned to England while he stayed behind to devote his energies to African exploration.

Over the years 1852-56 Livingstone became the first European to walk right across Africa. He was also the first European to see the great waterfalls known locally as "the smoke that thunders", which he renamed the Victoria Falls. The news of these great exploits quickly reached Britain and when he returned to England he was welcomed as a national hero and introduced to Queen Victoria.

In 1858 he organized an expedition to the Zambezi River, hoping that the presence of Europeans there would help to end the slave trade.

The *Ma-Robert* on the Zambezi.

But when his paddle steamer (the *Ma-Robert*) could not cross the rapids on the river, Livingstone abandoned the expedition and returned to England. He was back in Africa again in April 1866 and disappeared for three years. This time he was trying to find the source of the Nile (see page 10). Heading towards Lake Nyasa (Lake Malawi), he entered the heart of slaving country. He set up a base at Ujiji on the shores of Lake Tanganyika but the supplies he was expecting to find had been stolen and there was little to eat.

H.M. Stanley

John Rowlands was the real name of H.M. Stanley. He was born in Wales in 1841 and spent most of his unhappy childhood in an orphanage. As soon as he could he ran away and worked as a cabin boy on a ship bound for North America. There, at the age of 19, he was adopted by a cotton merchant from New Orleans. In gratitude he became an American citizen and took the name of his benefactor, Henry Morton Stanley.

Henry Stanley (1841-1904)

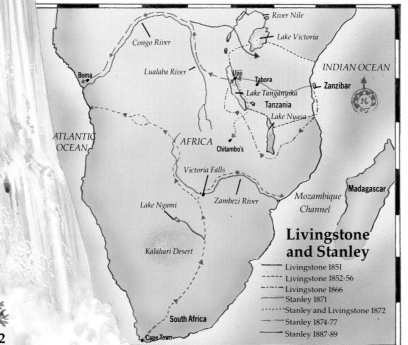

River Nile
Congo River
Lake Victoria
Lualaba River
Boma
Ujiji
Tabora
INDIAN OCEAN
Lake Tanganyika
Zanzibar
Tanzania
Lake Nyasa
ATLANTIC OCEAN
AFRICA
Chitambo's
Victoria Falls
Lake Ngami
Zambezi River
Mozambique Channel
Madagascar
Kalahari Desert

Livingstone and Stanley

Livingstone 1851
Livingstone 1852-56
Livingstone 1866
Stanley 1871
Stanley and Livingstone 1872
Stanley 1874-77
Stanley 1887-89

South Africa
Cape Town

Stanley's boat, the *Lady Alice*, could be taken apart and carried overland.

Travelling down the Lualaba River in the *Lady Alice*.

A new life in America

The young Stanley led an adventurous life in his adopted country. During the American Civil War of 1861-65, he fought first on one side and then the other. He later spent some time in the navy. Eventually he drifted into journalism and became a foreign correspondent for the *New York Herald*.

The search for Livingstone

In 1869 the owner of the newspaper commissioned Stanley to find out the fate of Livingstone, who had not been heard of since travelling into the interior of Africa three years earlier. At the beginning of 1871 Stanley arrived in Zanzibar. He immediately set about organizing one of the most expensive expeditions ever mounted with 192 of the best porters and the finest supplies.

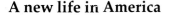

During the exhausting journey west, Stanley fell ill with malaria, his two European assistants died and

Stanley's hat and boots

the team was caught up in bloody battles between slave traders and African villagers. On 10 November 1871 they entered Ujiji. Stanley was led through the village by an excited crowd and, to his surprise and relief, he was introduced to the sick and frail Livingstone. Food and medicine soon restored Livingstone's strength and he and Stanley spent three weeks together exploring the northern end of Lake Tanganyika. At Tabora they parted company and Stanley returned to Zanzibar.

Stanley's meeting with Livingstone at Ujiji.

Livingstone's final journey

Before Stanley left Zanzibar for England, he sent new supplies to Livingstone. On 25 August 1872, Livingstone set out on his final journey, this time round the southern shores of Lake Tanganyika. Once more he caught a terrible fever, but at last he managed to reach a village in Ulala called Chitambo's. There he grew weaker and weaker and died eight months later. His heart was cut out by his faithful

Livingstone is carried dying into Chitambo's.

companions Chuma and Susi and buried under a tree. They then embalmed his body and carried it to Zanzibar, an eight-month journey of 1,609km (1,000 miles). From there it was shipped back to London and buried in Westminster Abbey. Livingstone is the only explorer to have received this honour.

Stanley returns to Africa

Inspired by his travels with Livingstone, Stanley returned to Africa in 1874, leading a huge expedition to map Lake Victoria and Lake Tanganyika. While out in their boats they were attacked by tribesmen and hippopotamuses and drenched by storms. However, the journey did establish that Lake Victoria had only one major inlet and one major outlet – the Nile. Speke's guess (see page 11) had been proved correct.

In October 1876 the group left Lake Tanganyika on its most exciting journey. Stanley intended to travel down the Lualaba River, following it wherever it went. All the way they were attacked by warriors. They entered dark, forbidding rainforests, where cannibals lived among the damp, dripping trees. At one point they walked along a road flanked by 186 human skulls.

The Lualaba flows into the Congo River and they sailed on down it until they finally arrived at Boma on the Atlantic coast. The last of Africa's great rivers had been conquered. Of the original 356 members of the expedition only 114 remained. The rest had either died or deserted and all three of Stanley's English assistants had died along the way.

The last exploration

In 1887 Stanley travelled once more to Africa on his final journey through the continent. He went to southern Sudan to rescue a German explorer called Emin Pasha who had become cut off from the outside world. The team of 700 men had to hack through some of the world's densest jungle. This was the last major exploration in Africa. It was no longer the mysterious continent it had once been and already the European powers were beginning to divide it up into colonies.

Stanley attacked by tribesmen.

East goes west

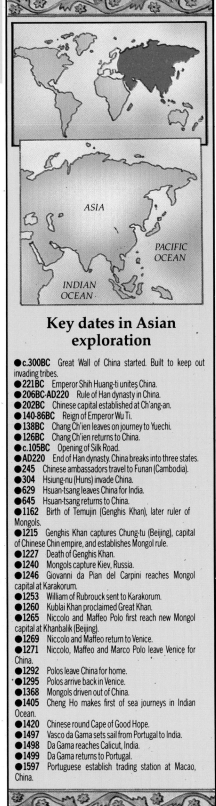

The ancient civilization of China evolved in isolation from those in the West, protected behind the barrier of deserts and mountains of central Asia. It was not until the 2nd century BC that people from China ventured to make their first contacts with the kingdoms and empires of the West.

Chang Ch'ien

During the 1st century BC, China's long borders were under attack from the Huns, fierce nomadic tribesmen from central Asia. The Emperor Wu Ti of China hoped to make an alliance with the Yuechi, a tribe who had been forced westwards by the Huns, against this threat. For this mission he chose an official called Chang Ch'ien.

Chang Ch'ien set off in 138BC on what turned out to be a very long journey. Almost immediately he was captured by the Huns and held prisoner. After ten years he eventually managed to escape and struggled to Heyuchi, the Yuechi capital lying close to the Khyber Pass.

But the Yuechi were not interested and Chang Ch'ien failed to win their support, so he set off on his return journey to China. This time he chose a roundabout route through Tibet to try to

A Chinese official and his attendants.

avoid the Huns. However, he fell into their hands once more. But he managed to escape and arrived back at Ch'ang-an, then the capital of China, after 12 years away and with just two of his original party of 100 men.

The Silk Road

Although Chang Ch'ien had failed in his mission, he learned a lot about the people and places he had seen along the way. This knowledge was used to open up the Silk Road, a trade route between China and the West. From about 105BC, long caravans of camels set out from China laden with bales of silk, spices, rare woods and resins, tortoiseshell, precious stones and pearls. They travelled through Asia to Antioch and then by ship to Rome.

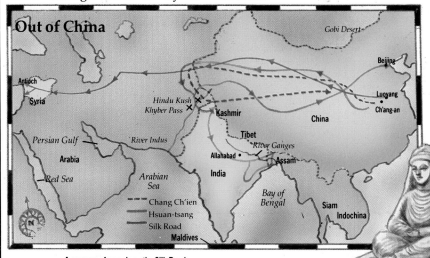

A caravan of camels on the Silk Road passes a statue of the Buddha at Luoyang, China.

Hsuan-tsang

One of the most adventurous travellers was a Buddhist monk called Hsuan-tsang. In AD629, against the emperor's strict instructions not to travel, he set out from China with the aim of learning more about his religion. His fortunes were to fluctuate from being honoured by kings to encounters with murderous brigands. His route to India, the birthplace of Buddhism, took him west through the Gobi Desert, along perilous roads and through dark gorges to Bactria, over the Hindu Kush and east into Kashmir. He remained studying for two years, visiting the libraries of monasteries in the Ganges valley.

Hsuan-tsang (c.602-664)

He visited Allahabad where he was captured by pirates and nearly sacrificed. In Assam he joined the procession of King Harsha, in the company of 20,000 elephants and 30,000 boats. While crossing the River Indus he lost many of his rare manuscripts and his entire collection of flower seeds. He set off north across the mountains, this time accompanied by an elephant with a huge appetite which ate 40 bundles of hay and hundreds of buns every day.

Despite all the perils, Hsuan-tsang finally arrived back in China after an absence of 16 years. He entered Ch'ang-an with a chariot drawn by 20 horses piled with 700 religious books, and statues and relics of the Buddha. His expedition was considered so important that, far from being reprimanded for disobeying the emperor's orders years before, he was showered with honours.

Cheng Ho

During the years following Hsuan-tsang's adventures, the Chinese established trade contacts with India. By the 8th century they had reached the Arabian peninsula and the east coast of Africa. Chinese coins and porcelain were exchanged for African gold, ivory, rhinoceros horns and precious woods and spices. In 1415 the Chinese emperor was delighted when ambassadors from Malindi presented him with a giraffe.

In 1368 the Mongols, who had ruled China for 150 years, were driven out. At the beginning of the 15th century the new Emperor Cheng Tsu planned a huge programme of exploration abroad. The man put in charge was a high-ranking courtier called Cheng Ho. He was in command of more than 27,000 men and a fleet of 317 ships.

Between 1405 and 1433, Cheng Ho made seven great voyages visiting, among other places, Indochina, Java, Sumatra, Siam (now Thailand), the Maldive Islands, Borneo, the Persian Gulf, Arabia and the east coast of Africa. Some of the ships were sent on surveying expeditions into the Pacific Ocean where they may even have reached the northern coast of Australia. Another group may also have rounded the Cape of Good Hope, for a Chinese map of about 1420 clearly shows part of Africa's west coast. This was 60 years before Bartolemeu Dias became the first European to round the Cape (see page 7).

Two years after Cheng Ho returned from his final expedition the last emperor of the Ming dynasty died. With him died the Chinese interest in exploration and a new foreign policy was adopted. They turned their backs on the outside world and stopped all exploration of the West.

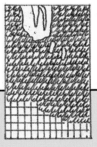

15th-century Chinese map showing the Cape of Good Hope at the top.

The Chinese junk

15th-century Chinese ships, called junks, were huge compared with European ones of the same period. Some of Cheng Ho's ships weighed more than ten times as much as Vasco da Gama's (see page 18).

Sea-going junks were designed with flat bottoms so that they could carry more cargo. There were special watertight compartments for the cargo.

Chinese junks were designed with three masts hundreds of years before European three-masted ships. The sails were square and staggered so that they all caught the wind.

Marco Polo

In the 13th century, a warrior tribe from northeast Asia called the Mongols, led by Genghis Khan, conquered huge areas of land in China and the Middle East. They reached as far west as Poland and Hungary.

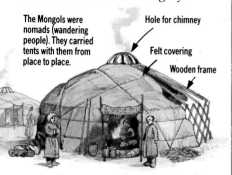

The Mongols were nomads (wandering people). They carried tents with them from place to place.

Hole for chimney

Felt covering

Wooden frame

At first, some European countries feared the Mongols would invade them too, leaving a trail of death and destruction. Once it became clear that this was not going to happen, however, Europe began to consider the Mongols as possible allies against their long-standing enemies, the Turks.

Ambassador priests

Several European countries sent ambassadors to the Mongol capital, Karakorum. In 1245 Pope Innocent IV sent a priest, Giovanni da Pian del Carpini, to meet the Great Khan (the Mongol leader). Later a monk, William of Rubrouck, made the same journey on behalf of the king of France. But both visits were diplomatic failures.

William of Rubrouck meeting the Great Khan

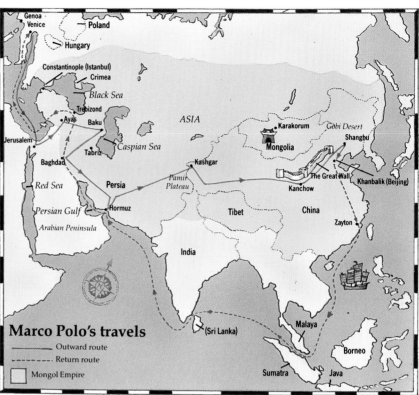

Marco Polo's travels

— Outward route

- - - - Return route

□ Mongol Empire

The triumph of trade

Carpini's route was later used by merchants. In the early 1260s the Venetian brothers Maffeo and Niccolo Polo, returning from a trade mission in the Crimea, found their way blocked by the Mongols. They made a lengthy detour, and on the way met a Mongol ambassador who invited them to China. They succeeded where the priests had not, and returned to Europe with a friendly letter for the Pope from Kublai Khan, the Mongol ruler in China.

Marco Polo's expedition

In 1271 the brothers set off for China again. This time they took with them Niccolo's son Marco, who was 15 years old. On the way they saw many amazing sights, such as a geyser pumping out hot oil, and large sheep with curly horns, each about 1.5m (4ft) in length. Marco noted many things, such as crafts and farming of the different areas, the people, and their religion and customs.

At Kublai Khan's court

Eventually, after three and a half years' travelling, the Polos reached Kublai Khan's court in Khanbalik (modern Beijing). They were again made welcome and Kublai Khan was particularly impressed by young Marco – so much so that he employed him as a representative of the imperial court. Marco went on many diplomatic missions, to such places as Malaya, Sumatra, Tibet and Sri Lanka, on behalf of Kublai Khan. He even recorded a journey to Burma and India.

Kublai Khan, the Mongol ruler of China, wearing Chinese imperial robes.

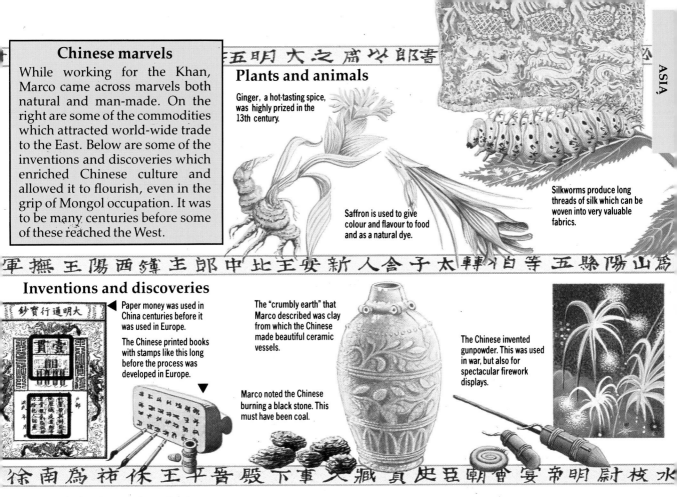

Chinese marvels

While working for the Khan, Marco came across marvels both natural and man-made. On the right are some of the commodities which attracted world-wide trade to the East. Below are some of the inventions and discoveries which enriched Chinese culture and allowed it to flourish, even in the grip of Mongol occupation. It was to be many centuries before some of these reached the West.

Plants and animals

Ginger, a hot-tasting spice, was highly prized in the 13th century.

Saffron is used to give colour and flavour to food and as a natural dye.

Silkworms produce long threads of silk which can be woven into very valuable fabrics.

Inventions and discoveries

Paper money was used in China centuries before it was used in Europe.

The Chinese printed books with stamps like this long before the process was developed in Europe.

The "crumbly earth" that Marco described was clay from which the Chinese made beautiful ceramic vessels.

Marco noted the Chinese burning a black stone. This must have been coal.

The Chinese invented gunpowder. This was used in war, but also for spectacular firework displays.

A final diplomatic mission

The Polos stayed in the service of Kublai Khan for 17 years. In 1292 they decided it was time to leave, but the Khan was reluctant to lose his loyal servants. A last diplomatic mission gave them an excuse: they were to return via Persia (now Iran), so that they could escort a Mongol princess to her husband-to-be, the Il-Khan Arghun. By the time they arrived, however, the Il-Khan had died. The Princess married his son instead.

The Polos sailed to Hormuz in Chinese boats called junks. From there they went by land to Trebizond and sailed back to Venice via

A Chinese town in the time of Marco Polo.

Constantinople. In all the journey took three years, and when they finally arrived back in Venice they had been away for 24 years. Marco was 39 when he returned. He married and became a merchant like his father and uncle.

Home to Venice

Settling in Venice again did not diminish Marco Polo's spirit of adventure. When Venice was at war with Genoa, he was taken prisoner while fighting for his city.

While in prison, Marco told his life story to his cell-mate, a writer called Rustichello. Rustichello later produced a book, *The Travels of Marco Polo*, which made his story famous all over the world.

Many of Marco's stories

seemed so far-fetched that people thought he had made them up. Some of his claims have never been verified. Although many merchants later followed the Polos' routes, they left no accounts of their travels to back up his claims. Marco's book inspired many later explorers, including Christopher Columbus (see page 22).

Marco Polo and Rustichello

The way east is closed

In 1368 the Chinese rebelled against the Mongols. They installed their own emperors who forbade visitors from Europe. Further west, some Mongols became Muslims and did not welcome Christians, so the landroute east from Europe was blocked again.

Vasco da Gama and the route to India

Having reached the Cape of Good Hope (see page 7), the Portuguese wanted to find a route around Africa to India. King Manuel I of Portugal chose a courtier called Vasco da Gama to lead an expedition to see if this route actually existed. Da Gama set sail in July 1497 with four ships and 170 men. Some of the men were convicts, recruited to do the most dangerous tasks. The king ordered da Gama to investigate any opportunities for trade along the way.

Vasco da Gama
(1460-1524)

Into the unknown

The man who had first rounded the Cape of Good Hope, Bartolemeu Dias, accompanied the new expedition in his own ship as far as the Cape Verde Islands. From here, da Gama and his fleet took four months to reach the Cape. They then sailed up the eastern coast of Africa. From time to time they landed to take food and water on board, to make repairs, and to trade.

Scurvy strikes

Many of the crew fell ill with scurvy, a disease caused by a deficiency of vitamin C. Victims grew weak, developing fever and blisters, and rarely survived the illness. So many of his men died that da Gama had to burn one of his ships because there were not enough sailors left to form a crew to operate it.

Rival traders

Further up the coast, da Gama reached the ports of Kilwa and Mombasa. But trade in this area was controlled by Arab merchants. They were hostile to da Gama, fearing he would disrupt their trade agreements with the Africans.

Da Gama's ship being attacked.

Some African rulers were unimpressed with da Gama's goods and refused to trade. Others were more aggressive. In Mombasa armed men tried to capture the Portuguese, who only just managed to escape.

Monsoon winds to Calicut

In nearby Malindi, the locals were more sympathetic. Da Gama hired an experienced guide to steer his ships cross the Indian Ocean. Driven by a seasonal wind called the monsoon, they made the crossing in just 23 days. They reached Calicut in India after a total of ten months at sea.

A long way home

Da Gama was welcomed by the Indian princes, but his goods did not compare with their magnificent wealth. He could only buy small amounts of spices. Again, Arab merchants in the area were hostile. After only three months da Gama and his men left India for Portugal. The voyage was three months longer than the outward journey.

Da Gama returns

When he reached home, da Gama received a hero's welcome. He had only acquired a few samples of goods, but these proved to the king that there were good trading opportunities in India. Da Gama's voyage opened up the route for many later traders from Portugal.

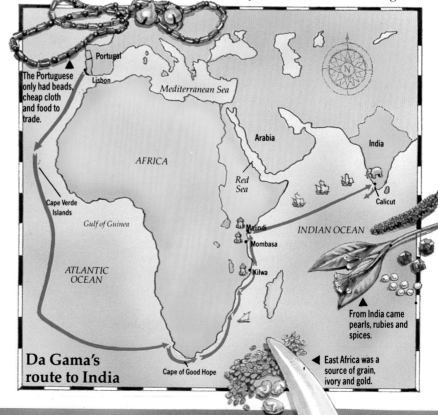

Portugal

The Portuguese only had beads, cheap cloth and food to trade.

Lisbon

Mediterranean Sea

Cape Verde Islands

Gulf of Guinea

ATLANTIC OCEAN

AFRICA

Red Sea

Arabia

India

Calicut

Malindi

Mombasa

INDIAN OCEAN

Kilwa

From India came pearls, rubies and spices.

East Africa was a source of grain, ivory and gold.

Cape of Good Hope

Da Gama's route to India

The search for the Northeast Passage

To compete with Portugal for eastern trade, northern European countries needed another sea route to the East. There were many attempts to find a Northeast Passage round northern Asia into the Pacific Ocean, and on to China and India.

Willem Barents

Barents, a Dutchman, made several voyages to find a way through to the East. In 1594 he sailed round the tip of Norway

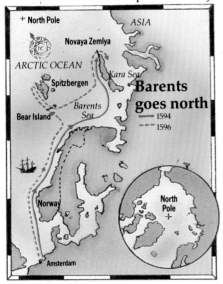

+ North Pole

ASIA

ARCTIC OCEAN

Novaya Zemlya

Kara Sea

Barents goes north

Spitzbergen

Barents Sea

— 1594

Bear Island

--- 1596

Norway

North Pole
+

Amsterdam

and reached the huge island of Novaya Zemlya. Here pack ice blocked his route and he had to turn back.

Trapped by ice

Barents sailed again in 1596. After reaching Spitzbergen he headed south and east to Novaya Zemlya once more. This time he sailed round its northernmost tip, but his ship became stuck in the ice. It was the beginning of the Arctic winter. Barents and his crew had no option but to build themselves a hut for shelter, and wait for warmer weather in the spring. Their ship was slowly crushed by the advancing ice, the timbers cracking.

A winter refuge

The hut was built from pieces of the wrecked ship. In 1871 a Norwegian fisherman found it, perfectly preserved by the ice.

Barents and his crew salvaged items which they could adapt for use on land. The crow's nest from the ship was put on top of the hut and used as a lookout tower.

The fisherman found books (including Barents' diary), a clock and cooking utensils.

A bath was adapted from a wooden barrel.

The ship's bunks were taken ashore and used as beds.

The front and side of the hut have been cut away in this picture to show the interior.

Surviving an Arctic winter

Barents and his men managed to survive the winter in their makeshift house. They killed bears and foxes for food, and burned polar bear fat and wood for light and heat. When the weather allowed, they played golf on the ice for exercise.

They suffered dreadfully from cold, hunger and scurvy. Even inside the hut the discomfort was hard to endure. The sheets froze on their beds and the smoke from the fire made it difficult to breathe.

When the Arctic spring came, and the ice began to melt, the expedition headed for home in the ship's two open boats. But for Barents, who was weakened by the rigours of the winter, the return journey proved too much. He had also fallen ill with scurvy and was so sickly he was unable to keep command of the boats. He grew weaker and weaker and died just five days after setting out for home, on Bear Island in the sea that is now named after him.

Polar bears often attacked the shelter.

Was there a way through?

Barents made great advances in Arctic exploration, but the Northeast Passage remained a mystery for centuries. Its existence was not proved until 1741, when a Dane, Vitus Bering, sailed through the narrow straits between Alaska and Asia which are now named after him. However the passage was far too dangerous and remote to be a good trade route.

The Vikings reach America

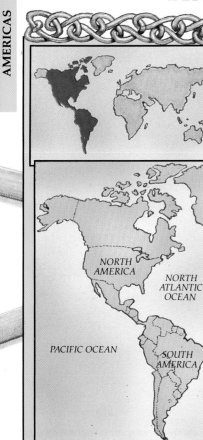

Key dates in American exploration

The Vikings were seafarers and warriors who had lived in Norway, Sweden and Denmark since ancient times. They began sailing west in the 9th century, searching for new territory. By about 860 some of them had reached Iceland and settled there. During their frequent journeys west, they became the first Europeans to discover America.

The Vikings were excellent metalworkers and used elaborately decorated swords like these.

Around 900, a ship commanded by a man called Gunnbjorn was sailing to Iceland from Norway. His ship was blown off course, and he saw a new land which he described to the settlers when he finally got to Iceland. His story inspired other Vikings to go in search of the new country.

Eric the Red

Eric the Red was a Norwegian who was banished from his country for three years for murder. He decided to use his period of exile to search for new lands to colonize, and set his sights in particular on the place that Gunnbjorn had spotted. After a hazardous voyage he arrived there but found that it had a hostile climate and landscape.

The Vikings' exploits were later recorded in long tales called sagas. This is a page from the saga about Eric the Red's discovery of Greenland.

Eric the Red wanted other Vikings to follow him there. He called the new country Greenland – not a very appropriate name for such unforgiving territory. By 986 he had convinced a group of colonists to settle there.

After a gruelling journey the expedition arrived in Greenland. It was summer, and conditions were favourable enough to establish farms. Settlements soon grew up, and the colonists were able to begin trading with Scandinavia.

Bjarni Herjolfsson

Soon another Norwegian, called Bjarni Herjolfsson, set out for Greenland, but went astray in fog and gales. He realized he had lost his way when land finally loomed out of the fog at him. It was not the harsh territory he had been told to expect when he reached Greenland. Instead it proved to be hilly and wooded.

In fact, the storms had blown Herjolfsson's ship far to the southwest of Greenland. We now know that the shoreline he saw was the northeastern coast of America. Instead of landing there, however, he turned back. When he finally reached Greenland, he reported his findings to the Viking colonists there.

A Viking warrior

A Viking ship

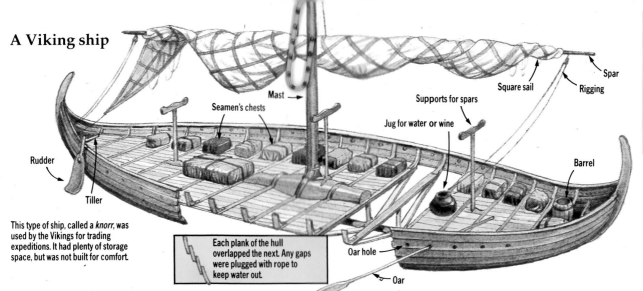

Rudder

Tiller

Seamen's chests

Mast →

Jug for water or wine

Supports for spars

Square sail

Rigging

Spar

Barrel

This type of ship, called a *knorr*, was used by the Vikings for trading expeditions. It had plenty of storage space, but was not built for comfort.

Each plank of the hull overlapped the next. Any gaps were plugged with rope to keep water out.

Oar hole

Oar

Leif Ericsson

The first European actually to set foot on American soil was Eric the Red's son, Leif Ericsson. Around the year 1000 he and his men left Greenland and sailed southwest. They landed at three places on the eastern coast of America. Leif gave these names: Markland ("forest land"; now the region of Labrador); Heluland ("slab-land", after the rocky landscape; now Baffin Island); and Vinland ("vine-land"; experts are unsure, but Vinland was probably where either New England or Newfoundland is now).

According to the saga of his voyage, Ericsson found wild grapes on the American coast, and the biggest fish he had ever seen.

Defeated by the Skraelings

Ericsson's men spent the winter in Vinland, then returned to Greenland with the news of their discovery. Although Leif himself never returned to the new lands, his brother Thorwald set out in 1002 to set up a colony there. He and his men found Vinland, but they were not prepared for the hostility of the native American Indians (known by the

Vikings as Skraelings). Thorwald was killed in a fight, and his companions returned to Greenland discouraged.

Eric the Red's descendants made two more attempts to colonize Vinland. The first expedition included his daughter-in-law Gudrid and her second husband. They settled there and started a family, and succeeded in trading successfully with the Skraelings. But later relations between settlers and natives deteriorated. The Vikings had to give up their home and return to Greenland. They finally settled in Iceland.

This is what a Skraeling warrior might have looked like.

A second expedition was led by Eric the Red's daughter Freydis, but she too failed to establish good relations with the Indians. She also caused chaos among her own people, and murdered several of her fellow colonists.

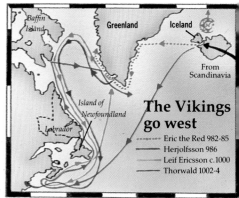

The Vikings go west

- - - - Eric the Red 982-85
——— Herjolfsson 986
——— Leif Ericsson c.1000
——— Thorwald 1002-4

The evidence

The theory that the Vikings had reached America was quite common for many years, but until the mid-1960s there was no reliable evidence. Doubts also arose when a map of the northeast coast, said to date from Viking times, turned out to be a fake. But in 1968 the remains of a Viking settlement were discovered in Newfoundland, proving that the Vikings had managed to reach America.

Fragments of Viking woodwork found at Newfoundland.

Christopher Columbus

Christopher Columbus is probably the most famous explorer of all. However his greatest discovery, the continent of America, was made by mistake.

Columbus (c.1451-1506) was given his own coat of arms in 1493, in honour of his discoveries.

Born in 1451 in Genoa, Italy, Columbus first went to sea as a young boy. He settled in Lisbon in 1479 and married the daughter of a Portuguese nobleman. From Lisbon he made various sea voyages, acquiring excellent skills as a navigator.

"Gold, God and Cathay"

Columbus's ambition was to sail to the Far East. His reasons are often summed up in the phrase "Gold, God and Cathay". The gold he had in mind was the fortune to be made bringing spices and silk home from China and Japan.

"God" refers to Columbus's wish to spread Christianity to non-Christian countries and to claim new lands in the name of God. This was a common motive among Europeans at that time. It was considered a worthy aim in itself, but

This Spanish gold cross symbolizes Columbus's motives for sailing to the Far East: spreading Christianity and making money.

Columbus hoped to find precious spices like cinnamon (left), nutmeg and peppercorns (below).

many explorers also saw another benefit. They thought that foreign trade would be easier with Christian countries.

"Cathay" was an ancient name for China. Columbus was obsessed with the Far East, and wanted to lead an expedition there.

Testing a theory

In the 15th century most people believed that the Earth was flat. Columbus, however, thought it was round. He hoped to prove this by sailing west to get to the Far East (see globe opposite), instead of taking the usual route from Europe, east round Africa.

Columbus took years to find money for his scheme, as few people believed it would work. Eventually, in 1492, Queen Isabella and King Ferdinand of Spain gave him the money he needed.

The voyage begins

Columbus left Spain on 3 August 1492 with three ships (see box). On 6 September they sailed from the Canary Islands out into open seas. At that time it was unusual to travel out of sight of the coast, and as days went by without a glimpse of land the crewmen became anxious. By the time they reached the strange, weed-infested Sargasso Sea, many of the men were desperate to turn back.

Many of Columbus's crew believed they were sailing into seas that were full of huge monsters.

Columbus persuaded them to go on by promising to give up if they did not sight land within a few days. But in his diary he recorded his intention to continue regardless of his men's desires.

Columbus's ships

These are the three ships that Spain provided for Columbus's voyage.

The Santa Maria

The Santa Maria was the fleet's largest ship, captained by Columbus himself.

The Niña

The Niña was smaller than the Santa Maria. The captain was Vicente Yanez Pinzón.

The Pinta

The Pinta was similar to the Niña. Pinzón's brother, Martín Alonzo Pinzón, was its captain.

Between them the ships carried 104 men and vast quantities of supplies, including live pigs and chickens, salted meat, flour, rice, wine and water. There was also equipment for repairing the ships.

Land ahoy!

On 12 October, the lookout on the *Pinta* saw land. It was what is now called Watling Island in the Bahamas, off the coast of America. Columbus, however, was convinced he had reached Cathay. As he had wildly underestimated how long it would take him to reach the Far East, he was not at all surprised to find land when he did. He would not accept his mistake as long as he lived, and never realized the significance of his discovery.

Columbus's route would have worked if America had not been in his path.

------ Intended route

------ Actual route

Columbus named the island San Salvador. The inhabitants were friendly, and eager to trade. Columbus found little evidence of the riches of the East, but he was still certain that he was near his goal. Guided by the local people, he led the fleet onward in search of Cathay and its treasures.

He visited Cuba, then an island which he named La Española (now Hispaniola). He was then impatient to return to Spain to report his findings.

This woodcut, from the 1493 edition of Columbus's journals, shows some of the islands he visited.

The Allegory of Discovery

This Spanish gold shield, known as the Allegory of Discovery, was made in the 16th century. By this time the Spanish had understood the full importance of Columbus's achievements.

Neptune, the Greek god of the sea.

This figure represents Columbus.

The 'horn of plenty' – a symbol of the rich natural resources that explorers found on the American continent.

Disaster and triumph

On Christmas Day 1492, the *Santa Maria* was wrecked at La Española when it hit a reef. Columbus had to leave 43 men behind, as there was no room on the other ships. He was welcomed as a hero when he reached Spain. The islands he had found became known as "the Indies", as people thought they were off the coast of Asia in the Indian Ocean.

A second expedition

In 1493 Columbus led a new fleet to the Indies, but his visit was not a success. Firstly he found at La Española that the men he had left behind had been killed by the islanders. Then he formed a new settlement, but governed it badly, brutally mistreating the natives and Spaniards alike.

Columbus disgraced

News of Columbus's behaviour had reached Spain when he returned in 1496. Although the king and queen were angry, they let him go back to the Indies in 1498. But further unrest there alarmed Ferdinand and Isabella, and they appointed a new governor.

When Columbus reached Cuba having failed to calm a revolt on La Española, he was arrested by the governor and sent back to Spain in chains. Isabella later forgave him, but his pride was badly wounded. He claimed he had been misunderstood, and asked to be buried with the chains as a reminder of the way he had been treated.

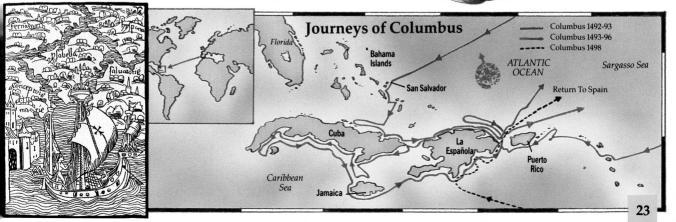

Journeys of Columbus

— Columbus 1492-93
— Columbus 1493-96
--- Columbus 1498

Florida

Bahama Islands

San Salvador

ATLANTIC OCEAN

Sargasso Sea

Return To Spain

Cuba

La Española

Puerto Rico

Caribbean Sea

Jamaica

Cortés

Columbus's death marks a turning point in the history of European exploration. Before that most explorers were professional navigators and seamen employed by monarchs. Though they wanted personal profit from their voyages, they had other, more long-term aims. These included finding trade routes for their patrons and taking Christianity to non-Christian countries. In the 16th century, new, more ruthless explorers became common. They are known as conquistadors, after the Spanish word for "conquerors".

Cortés
1485-1547

The conquistadors

At the turn of the century an Italian explorer, Amerigo Vespucci, sailed to the land Columbus had found and established that it was an entirely new continent. In 1507 this "New World", as it was known, was named America, after Vespucci.

The conquistadors were Spanish adventurers and soldiers. They believed America and its resources were there to be taken regardless of who lived there. In conquering the new lands many of them remorselessly wiped out whole civilizations.

Cortés sails to the New World

Hernándo Cortés was born in 1485 to a distinguished but poor Spanish family. He first studied law, but soon found he was more attracted to the excitement of a soldier's life. His first major expedition was with Diego Velazquez, a conquistador who set out in 1511 to seize Cuba. When Velazquez succeeded, Cortés did well out of the conquest. He was soon a rich and important man, and for a time he was even Mayor of Cuba's capital Santiago. Soon, however, rumours of an empire rich in gold on the American mainland aroused his curiosity, and he set off in search of it.

The Aztec empire

The Aztecs were American Indians who lived in what is now Mexico. Their civilization began in about 1325, when they arrived in the area from further north and began building their capital city Tenochtitlán. Aztec culture was highly sophisticated in many areas, especially science, art, architecture and agriculture. The Aztecs had their own mode of picture writing and a great many laws and elaborate religious rites and ceremonies. They were also highly skilled jewellers and weavers.

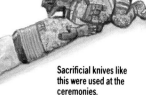

Sacrificial knives like this were used at the ceremonies.

Human sacrifices

One of the most shocking Aztec customs was the ritual of human sacrifice. The Aztecs believed their sun god, Huitzilpochtli, died each night, and would only be reborn the next day if he was nourished with a constant supply of human blood. Thousands of victims were brutally sacrificed each year. They were often slaves or prisoners of war, but sometimes Atzecs themselves. Many had their hearts cut out while they were still living.

The heads of victims were kept on skull racks like this.

Towards Tenochtitlán

In 1519 Cortés left Santiago, intending to make his fortune by conquering the Aztecs. He sailed for the American mainland with

Shrine to the sun god

Sacrificial altar

This is what an Aztec temple might have looked like.

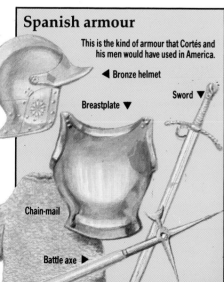

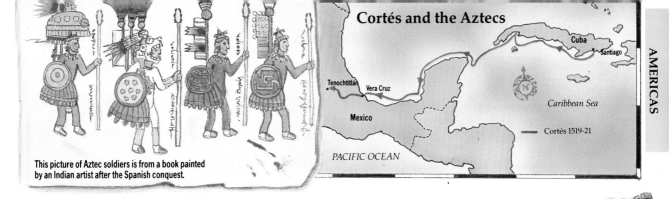

Serpent-shaped
Aztec pendant inlaid with turquoise

This picture of Aztec soldiers is from a book painted by an Indian artist after the Spanish conquest.

600 men, 16 horses and several cannons. After founding the city of Vera Cruz on the coast, he continued inland towards Tenochtitlán.

The Aztecs had recently conquered several rival tribes in the area and had made many enemies. Malinche, the daughter of one tribal chief, fell in love with Cortés and offered to accompany him on his journey as a guide and interpreter. (The Spaniards named her Dona Mariña.) Her services were crucial in gaining support from the other Indian tribes for his invasion of the Aztecs.

Mask of Quetzalcoatl (see below).

Warrior gods

The Aztecs were terrified by Cortés's cannons and horses. Some thought his arrival was the god Quetzalcoatl returning to Earth, as predicted in an Aztec myth. But their emperor Montezuma thought otherwise. Astrologers had spoken of an invasion and the downfall of the Aztec Empire, and he worried that the predictions were coming true. To put the Spaniards off their guard, he treated them like the gods his people took them for, kissing the ground before their feet and giving them precious gifts.

Montezuma's downfall

Montezuma's attempt to pacify the Spaniards did him no good. Cortés took him prisoner and demanded a huge ransom of gold. The gold was paid, but Cortés cheated the Aztecs and kept Montezuma captive.

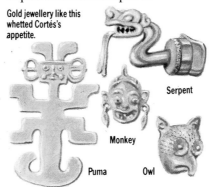
Gold jewellery like this whetted Cortés's appetite.

Serpent

Monkey

Puma   Owl

Then news reached Cortés that a rival in Vera Cruz had challenged his authority. He rushed to the coast to deal with the problem, and returned to find that one of his men had staged an unprovoked attack on an Aztec religious meeting and killed many of the participants.

The Aztecs were in uproar, so Cortés produced Montezuma, hoping to calm the rioters. But the former ruler had never been popular, and the sight of him enraged the crowds even more. They stoned him to death then turned on the Spaniards.

Cortés's men suffered heavy losses in the fighting and withdrew to the protection of friendly tribes nearby. Then in August 1521, Cortés besieged Tenochtitlán. Food and water were cut off for nearly three months. Countless Aztecs died. Some starved, but many caught smallpox which the Spanish had unknowingly brought with them from Europe.

An empire destroyed

After the fall of Tenochtitlán, the Aztec Empire was rapidly destroyed. The Indians had no immunity to European diseases, so millions of them died. In addition many conquistadors were brutal rulers. Within a few years of Montezuma's death, little of the Aztec world remained.

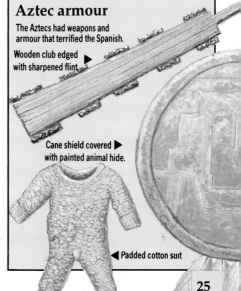

Aztec armour

The Aztecs had weapons and armour that terrified the Spanish.

▶ Wooden club edged with sharpened flint.

▶ Cane shield covered with painted animal hide.

◀ Padded cotton suit

The hunt for the Northwest Passage

Like the Spanish, the British and French were also keen to reach the riches of the East by sailing west. Rather than following the Spanish routes round South America (see pages 38-39), they sought a new route round North America. They were sure that they would find a channel through which their ships could sail. This was known as the Northwest Passage.

Frobisher meets the challenge

An English expedition to find the Northwest Passage was organized by the navigator Sir Humphrey Gilbert. Three ships set sail from London in 1576 under the command of a captain called Martin Frobisher.

Martin Frobisher (1535-94)

The coast of Greenland was blocked by ice and Frobisher's ship lost its mast in a gale. But he repaired the damage and continued with his journey. Believing he had found the approach to the Northwest Passage, he named it Frobisher's Strait, without realizing it was only an inlet (now Frobisher Bay) that led nowhere.

Encounter with the Inuit

While he was exploring the inlet, Frobisher was met by Inuit (the local inhabitants). They skimmed across the water in one-man canoes called kayaks and surrounded Frobisher's ship.

Kayaks are made from wooden frames covered with sealskins.

Wooden frame

Sealskin covering

Paddle →

When Frobisher first saw a kayak from a distance, he thought it was a seal or a large fish.

Kidnap

The Inuit seemed friendly and traded food and furs. But five of the crew were kidnapped when they left their ship. Frobisher captured an Inuit as a hostage against the return of his sailors, but they were never seen again. The Inuit was taken back to England, where he died of pneumonia.

The search for gold

One of the crew went ashore and brought back some black rocks streaked with glittering gold veins. When Frobisher returned to London experts declared that the rocks contained gold. On his next two voyages to the region in 1577 and 1578, Frobisher collected huge quantities of the rocks. When he returned home after the final journey, he was told that the rocks he had collected were worthless. They had been identified as iron pyrites, also known as "fool's gold".

Iron pyrites or "fool's gold".

The quest continues

The failure to find the elusive Northwest Passage did not discourage others from making the attempt. John Davis, who discovered the Davis Strait, made three voyages between 1585 and 1587.

In 1610 Henry Hudson sailed along the north coast of Canada in a ship called the *Discovery*. But his crew, convinced he had a secret hoard of food, cast him adrift with his son and a few loyal sailors. Hudson was lost forever in the bay that now bears his name.

In 1616 William Baffin and Robert Bylot sailed up the Davis Strait as far as Smith Sound, which would have taken them through to open sea, but the icy weather forced them to turn back. The Northwest Passage remained uncharted for centuries. It was finally navigated by Roald Amundsen (see pages 40-41).

An Inuit hunting bow made out of walrus-tusk ivory.

Carvings of hunting scenes

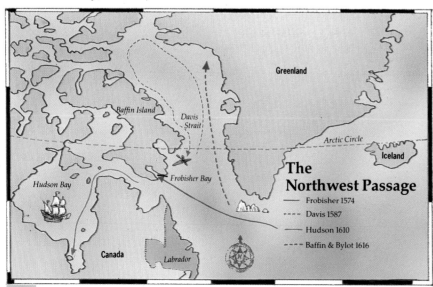

Greenland

Baffin Island

Davis Strait

Arctic Circle

Iceland

Hudson Bay

Frobisher Bay

The Northwest Passage

—— Frobisher 1574
---- Davis 1587
—— Hudson 1610
---- Baffin & Bylot 1616

Canada

Labrador

The building of New France

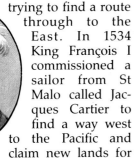

Jacques Cartier
(1491-1557)

W hile the English were enduring the miseries of the freezing Arctic waters, the French were also trying to find a route through to the East. In 1534 King François I commissioned a sailor from St Malo called Jacques Cartier to find a way west to the Pacific and claim new lands for France.

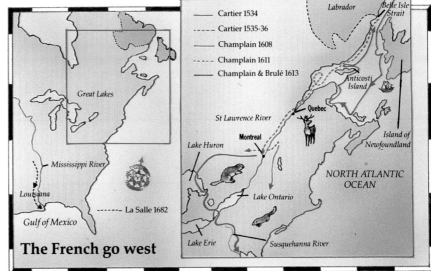

The French go west

Missed opportunities

Cartier's expedition set out in two ships from St Malo in 1534. He headed for Newfoundland and then sailed through the Belle Isle Strait, noting that the rocky shores would be of no use to settlers. Rounding Anticosti Island, he sighted the mouth of the St Lawrence River. Mistaking it for a bay, he failed to investigate it and returned to France.

Help from the Indians

Cartier left on a second voyage in May 1535 and reached Belle Isle Strait at the end of July. He acquired two guides from the Huron tribe who led his party up the St Lawrence River. They passed the small native village of Stadacona (later Quebec), then pressed on upstream through the rapids to a town called Hochelaga where they met the Huron chief, Donnaconna. Cartier named a nearby hill Mont Réal (Mount Royal), which later became the site of the city of Montreal.

Cartier and his men spent a terrible winter at Stadacona, suffering from scurvy and extreme cold. On 6 May 1536 they finally sailed for home. On the way they

kidnapped Donnaconna to try to get him to reveal the whereabouts of gold mines. He was taken back to France, where he later died.

In the wake of Cartier

With wars raging in Europe, French kings lost interest in the New World for a time. However small groups of Frenchmen continued to follow Cartier's route up the St Lawrence and spread out along the many waterways. They learned how to survive in the wilderness, build birch-bark canoes and trap beavers and other animals for their fur. They established a trade network with the American Indians, which flourished rapidly. At the same time they were gradually building up an empire for France.

French explorers encountered many animals which they trapped for their fur and hide. ▶

The French empire grows

Samuel de Champlain, the French Royal Geographer, founded Quebec in 1608 and Montreal in 1611, strengthening France's hold in North America. In 1613 he was joined by Etienne Brulé who later reached the Susquehanna River.

In 1678 King Louis XIV sent an explorer called Robert de La Salle to build a chain of trading forts across the continent. La Salle followed the Mississippi River, reaching the Gulf of Mexico in 1682. He named the lands he passed through Louisiana after the king.

Elk

Otter

Beaver

Marten

Cartier travelled by canoe with Indian guides up the St Lawrence River.

Across the continent

By the mid-18th century there were so many new immigrants entering North America from Europe that the original colonies in the Northeast were overcrowded. Expansion was difficult as the settlers were afraid to venture west into the unknown lands over the Appalachian Mountains.

In 1803 the United States government bought the state of Louisiana from France. This prompted Thomas Jefferson, the American president, to plan an expedition to explore the lands beyond the Mississippi. This was mainly to assess opportunities for trade with American Indians and Mexicans, but also to find a route to the Pacific Ocean.

The team departs

The leaders of the expedition were Captain Meriwether Lewis, the president's private secretary, and Lieutenant William Clark. Lewis chose all the equipment needed, while Clark recruited

William Clark
(1770-1838)

Meriwether Lewis
(1774-1809)

and trained the men. The team of 30 men was known as the Corps of Discovery and left St Louis in a blaze of publicity on 14 May 1804, sailing up the River Missouri. As well as the usual equipment such as rifles, medicines and food supplies, they carried with them many trinkets as presents for the Indians.

An air-gun used on the expedition

Clark's pocket compass

Entering new lands

The two leaders made many notes on the profusion of plants and animals they saw along the way. Lewis complained of the terrible weather and the swarms of mosquitoes that plagued them throughout the night and day.

Prairie dog

Lewis's woodpecker

Mountain flower

After eleven weeks they encountered the Oto, Missouri and Omaha tribes of Indians. They exchanged gifts and made peace and trade treaties with them. Then, moving deeper into the plains, they met about a thousand members of the Teton Sioux who made the team take part in a peace-pipe ceremony before allowing them to cross their lands.

Moving on

They reached an area now part of North Dakota where they set up camp and built a log fort. They spent the bitter winter there among the Mandan tribe. The team resumed its journey in the

A barge similar to the one used by Lewis and Clark

spring, travelling by barge up the Missouri. Gradually the currents ran stronger and the journey became more difficult, but by the end of May they were in sight of the majestic, snow-covered Rocky Mountains. Here they came across grizzly bears and were surprised by the power and ferocity of these huge animals that frequently attacked the party.

The explorers were often powerless when attacked by bears.

A way through the Rockies

Next, they had to find a way round the Great Falls on the Missouri as they could go no further. The task of moving the equipment round the falls took nearly a month and exhausted the men. By August they entered the lands of the Shoshoni Indians and here they encountered more difficulties, for they had underestimated the height of the Rockies. But they were helped by Sacagewea, the Shoshoni Indian wife of a Canadian interpreter in the party. She showed them the Lemhi Pass and guided them towards the Columbia River. They made contact with Sacagewea's people and were given new horses to continue their journey.

Sacagewea

Ocean in view!

The western face of the Rockies was very steep, criss-crossed by roaring waterfalls and slippery precipices. The going was tough,

Crossing the Rockies

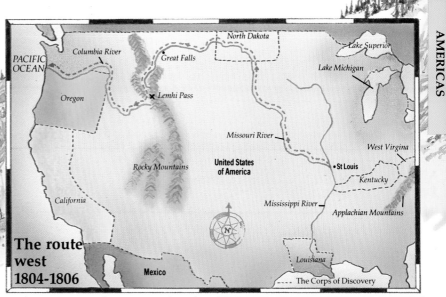

The route west 1804–1806

PACIFIC OCEAN

Columbia River

Great Falls

North Dakota

Lake Superior

Lake Michigan

Oregon

× Lemhi Pass

Missouri River

West Virginia

Rocky Mountains

United States of America

• St Louis

Kentucky

California

Mississippi River

Applachian Mountains

Louisiana

Mexico

- - - - The Corps of Discovery

food was in short supply and the nights were bitterly cold. They passed through the lands of the Chinook, the Clatsops and the majestic Nez Percé tribe, and finally reached the Columbia River. They paddled towards the coast, and on 7 November heard the roar of the Pacific breakers and smelled the sea-salt in the air. They climbed to the top of the final hill and saw the ocean spread before them. At last they had reached their goal.

The journey home

Winter was now closing in, so they built a camp which they named Fort Clatsop. From there they could watch the Pacific to hail any passing ship that might carry them back east. But nothing appeared on the horizon, so the team packed up and on 23 March set off on their six-month return journey to St Louis. Although they now knew the way, it was as exhausting as the outward trek. Also, conflict with the Blackfoot Indians caused difficulties which were to plague pioneers for many years. On 20 September 1806 they reached a French settlement where they saw the first Europeans for over two years.

A triumphant return

On 23 September 1806 they finally arrived back at St Louis after a journey of over 12,000km (7,456 miles) and an absence of two-and-a-half years. They had been gone for so long that many thought they must be dead. But Lewis and Clark had accomplished all they had set out to do. Most importantly, they had discovered a way to the West which gave access to the rest of the continent and the Pacific. They had also established good relations with many of the Indian tribes and opened up new trade routes.

The rush West

This mammoth expedition by the Corps of Discovery was followed by a new wave of explorers, mainly fur trappers known as "mountain men" who spilled over the mountains to make their fortunes. Further south, the Santa Fe, the Old Spanish, the Oregon and the Californian trade routes were established between the United States and Mexico.

Farmers and gold prospectors

Where the traders went, the farmers followed. In 1843 a group of settlers travelled west to Oregon in a thousand-strong wagon-train. When gold was discovered in California in 1849, a huge rush to the West began. Thousands of people left the East for the new lands, braving incredible hardship and the growing hostility of the Indians who realized that the settlers threatened their territory and way of life.

Mountain man in search of furs.

Gold nuggets from California.

A member of the party being attacked by Blackfoot Indians.

Scientists and dreamers

The first Europeans to explore and colonize South America in the 16th and 17th centuries were treasure hunters and missionaries. But during the 18th century many of the explorers were scientists. They were more interested in mapping the continent and in studying its geology and plant and animal life. The first such scientific expedition travelled to Peru in 1735.

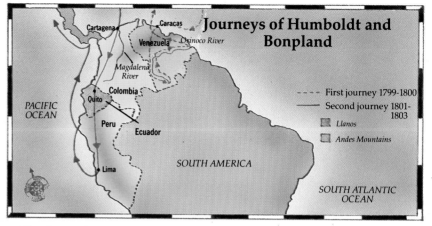

Journeys of Humboldt and Bonpland

- - - - First journey 1799-1800
———— Second journey 1801-1803
Llanos
Andes Mountains

Alexander von Humboldt

One of the greatest scientific explorers was a German called Alexander von Humboldt. As well as being a brilliant naturalist, he was an astronomer, biologist and geologist and also an expert linguist. In June 1797 Humboldt left his home in Berlin for Paris. In June 1799 he and a French doctor called Aimé Bonpland sailed from Europe to South America, reaching the north east coast near Caracas in present-day Venezuela the following month.

Alexander von Humboldt
(1769-1859)

Aimé Bonpland
(1773-1858)

One of their first projects was to explore the Orinoco River. But in order to reach it, they first had to cross the dry, baking and dusty plains called the *llanos* stretching to the south.

▲ The Incas were very skilled stonemasons. They cut the stones so accurately that they fitted perfectly.

All along the way they made detailed records of the many plants, animals and birds they saw and the country through which they passed – scorching deserts that parched their throats and dried up their skin. They travelled along winding rivers through hot steamy jungles, the silence pierced by the shrieks of parrots and monkeys, where they were plagued by swarms of blood-sucking insects.

Up mountains, down south

They made a second journey to South America in 1801 and reached Quito (one of the highest cities in the world) in January 1802, after an exhausting voyage along rivers and over mountains. Outside the city they climbed 5,878m (19,285ft) almost to the top of a volcanic peak called Chimborazo. Then they travelled south through lush forests and across the chilly slopes of the Andes Mountains until they reached Lima, Peru. Here they studied the archaeological remains of the Inca civilization. (The Incas flourished in Peru from the 13th century, but were wiped out by Spanish conquistadors (see page 24) in the 1530s.)

Humboldt also recorded the steady, cold current which flows along the Peruvian coast and is rich in stocks of fish. It was later named the Humboldt Current (now known as the Peru Current).

Back in Europe

Great crowds turned out to welcome the two explorers on their return to France in 1804. They had travelled 64,000km (40,000 miles) in South America and collected 30 chests of specimens and 60,000 plants, many of which were unknown before. Humboldt returned to Germany and spent the next 23 years preparing all their work for publication which eventually filled 29 volumes.

Bonpland identified thousands of plants for the first time.

Humboldt and Bonpland at the foot of Mount Chimborazo. ▼

Charles Darwin

Charles Darwin was an English naturalist and explorer. He joined a ship called the *Beagle* in December 1831 on a five-year expedition to map the coast of Chile. He made copious notes on all he saw, and although there was little room on the ship he built up a huge collection of rocks, fossils, plants, birds, animals and shells. The sights he saw and the observations he made would later lead him to challenge the traditional beliefs about how life on Earth began and evolved.

Charles Darwin (1809-82)

The land of giants

The expedition reached Bahia in Brazil in the spring of 1832. Darwin was amazed by the number and dazzling colours of the flowers and birds he saw. The Beagle sailed south along the coast of Patagonia where the crew discovered the fossil remains of several extinct animals, including a giant sloth and armadillo.

This is how the giant sloth and the armadillo might have looked.

They travelled to the bleak and wind-swept lands of Tierra del Fuego, at the very tip of South America. Darwin made a journey inland to the plains of Argentina known as the *pampas*, living among the *gauchos* (cowboys).

Darwin on a plant-hunting expedition.

A world apart

In September 1835 the expedition reached the strange, remote Galapagos Islands, lying 965km (600 miles) off the coast of Ecuador in the Pacific Ocean. There Darwin saw birds, animals and plants that are found nowhere else on Earth. Cut off from the mainland they had developed in isolation from their relations in America. They were to play an important part in Darwin's theories on how animals and humans evolve (see below).

These animals are ▶ only found on the Galapagos Islands.

The Bible is questioned

The *Beagle* reached England in October 1836 and Darwin spent over 20 years writing up his findings. In 1859 he published *The Origin of Species*, which set out his theories on evolution. These turned the teachings of the Church upside down. One of Darwin's most revolutionary theories was that all living things had evolved over many millions of years. This caused uproar, because it questioned the biblical idea that the world was created in six days and had remained unchanged since then.

Giant tortoise

Marine iguana

Galapagos finch

Percy Fawcett

Percy Fawcett was an army officer and surveyor with 20 years' experience of travel in South America. Inspired by the legend of El Dorado, "the golden man", he believed that somewhere deep in the Brazilian jungle lay the remains of a fabulous civilization. Near Salvador (Bahia) in 1921 he found remains which encouraged him and he intended to prove his theory by finding one of the lost cities, which he called "Z".

Percy Fawcett (1867-1925)

An unsolved mystery

On 20 April 1925, Fawcett set off with his eldest son Jack and a school friend of Jack's called Raleigh Rimell. They followed piranha-infested rivers into the Mato Grosso region of Brazil, and were never seen again. Over the following years rumours of what had happened to them came out of the jungle. They were probably killed by Indians, but nothing could be proved and their disappearance remains as much a mystery as Fawcett's fabled city.

SOUTH AMERICA
Ecuador
Brazil
Bahia (Salvador)
Galapagos Islands
Mato Grosso
PACIFIC OCEAN
Chile
Darwin and Fawcett
Argentina
Pampas
SOUTH ATLANTIC OCEAN
Patagonia
Darwin 1831-1835
Fawcett 1925
Tierra del Fuego — Cape Horn

The quest for a southern continent

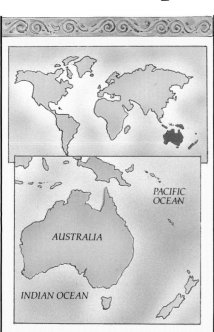

PACIFIC OCEAN

AUSTRALIA

INDIAN OCEAN

Key dates in Australasian exploration

- **1565** Andres de Urdaneta crosses the Pacific Ocean.
- **1606** Pedro Fernandes de Quiros reaches the New Hebrides Islands.
- **1606** Willem Jantszoon becomes the first European to reach Australia.
- **1642** Abel Tasman sights an island off the southern coast of Australia and names it Van Dieman's Land after Anthony van Dieman, Governor-General of the Dutch East Indies. It is now known as Tasmania.
- **1721** Jakob Roggeveen discovers Easter Island, on Easter Sunday.
- **1769** James Cook sails in the *Endeavour* to Tahiti and makes observations of Venus. He sails onto New Zealand where he discovers the east coast.
- **1770** Cook lands in Botany Bay, Australia.
- **1772** Cook's second voyage leaves Plymouth.
- **1774** Cook crosses Latitude 70° and the Antarctic Circle.
- **1776** Cook sets sail on his third voyage. Its main purpose was to find a route through the Northwest Passage from west to east.
- **1779** Cook sails to the Sandwich Islands (Hawaiian Islands) where he is killed.
- **1785** Jean François de la Pérouse leaves France in search of the Solomon Islands.
- **1788** De la Pérouse lands at Port Jackson, New South Wales, Australia.
- **1795** Mathew Flinders and George Bass make the first inland expedition from the east coast of Australia.
- **1801-2** Flinders carries out a survey of nearly all of the Australian coastline.
- **1828** Charles Sturt and Hamilton Hume cross the Blue Mountains, Australia.
- **1860** Robert Burke leads expedition from Melbourne to cross Australia from south to north.
- **1861** John Stuart leads second, rival expedition north across Australia from Adelaide.
- **1861** Death of Charles Gray, William Wills and Burke.
- **1862** Stuart returns south, having completed his crossing of Australia.

In 1565 a Spanish monk called Andres de Urdaneta made the first crossing of the Pacific. His account of the journey led many people to believe that a great southern continent lay somewhere to the west of the tip of South America. In 1606 Pedro Fernandes de Quiros, a Portuguese captain working for Spain, reached land he believed to be that continent. He named it "Australia" (after the King of Spain who was also Archduke of Austria), but it was in fact one of the islands now called the New Hebrides.

Discovery of a new continent

By the end of the 16th century, the Dutch were a powerful trading nation. In 1606 a Dutch captain from Amsterdam, Willem Jantszoon, became the first European to reach Australia. He sailed into the Gulf of Carpentaria on the northern coast. In 1642, another Dutchman, Abel Tasman, sighted the island that is now called Tasmania. He named it Van Diemen's Land after the governor of his employers, the Dutch East India Company. Tasman went on to discover New Zealand, then stopped at Tonga and Fiji. After this, Dutch interest in exploration dwindled. It was more than a hundred years before Australia was further explored.

Captain Cook

James Cook was born in Yorkshire, England. The son of a farm labourer, he received a very limited education at the local school. He began work when he was 12, first in a shop, then with a shipping company. In 1756 he joined the navy as a sailor.

James Cook (1728-79)

Cook was a very tall man, with a strong character and great intelligence. He was a gifted navigator and astronomer and in 1768 was appointed a lieutenant and given command of his first ship, the *Endeavour*.

The fight against disease

In the 18th century an average of 60 out of every 100 seamen died on long voyages, 50 of them from disease. Cook tried to reduce illness by introducing rigid rules. The men had to bathe every day. Their clothing and bedding were aired twice a week and the ship was regularly fumigated.

Cook took large quantities of fresh fruit on board ship. This was to prevent scurvy, a disease caused by a lack of vitamin C and one of the main causes of death among sailors. He also ensured that fresh meat and vegetables were obtained wherever possible. These measures improved the health of the sailors.

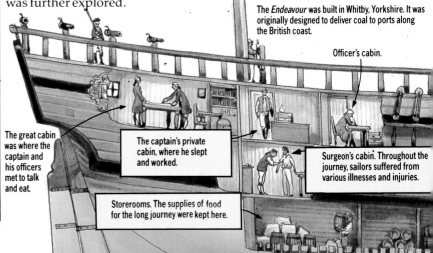

The *Endeavour* was built in Whitby, Yorkshire. It was originally designed to deliver coal to ports along the British coast.

Officer's cabin.

The great cabin was where the captain and his officers met to talk and eat.

The captain's private cabin, where he slept and worked.

Surgeon's cabin. Throughout the journey, sailors suffered from various illnesses and injuries.

Storerooms. The supplies of food for the long journey were kept here.

The men and the mission

In keeping with the scientific spirit of the times, Cook's first mission was to take his ship to Tahiti to observe the planet Venus as it passed between the Earth and the sun in 1769. Travelling with him on this voyage were a naturalist, a botanist and two artists. Cook carried with him a sealed envelope, to be opened after the observations had been recorded. It contained secret orders to seek out the fifth continent, to allow the scientists to study the plants, animals and native peoples, and to claim the land for Britain.

The expedition reached the island of Tahiti in April 1769. The scientists made their observations of Venus on 3 June and set sail again ten days later. Two of the islanders went with them as guides to help the expedition explore smaller islands nearby.

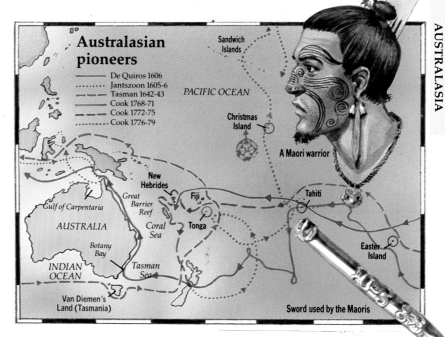

Australasian pioneers

—— De Quiros 1606
········· Jantszoon 1605-6
– – Tasman 1642-43
— — Cook 1768-71
— — Cook 1772-75
········· Cook 1776-79

Sandwich Islands
PACIFIC OCEAN
Christmas Island
A Maori warrior
New Hebrides
Fiji
Tahiti
Gulf of Carpentaria
Great Barrier Reef
Coral Sea
Tonga
AUSTRALIA
Botany Bay
Easter Island
INDIAN OCEAN
Tasman Sea
Van Diemen's Land (Tasmania)
Sword used by the Maoris

Breadfruit

Butterfly fish

The ships moved on to New Zealand, where they had a hostile reception from the Maoris. Fighting broke out and at one point the *Endeavour* was chased by about a hundred warriors in canoes.

Run aground

In April 1770 Cook landed at an inlet on the east coast of Australia. He named it Botany Bay after the many botanical specimens found there. Following the coast north, the ship was damaged when it ran into coral on the Great Barrier Reef. Once repairs were complete they set sail again and finally reached home in July 1771.

Cook's last voyages

Cook led two more expeditions, making further discoveries. The first set sail in two ships from Plymouth in July 1772. In January 1774 Cook and his crew crossed the Latitude 70°, the furthest south yet reached by Europeans, and visited Easter Island.

In 1779 Cook travelled to the Sandwich Islands (now the Hawaiian Islands). At first the Hawaiians treated him like a god, but they soon grew tired of their visitors. Cook set sail but returned six days later when his ship, the *Resolution,* suffered storm damage. A fight broke out and Cook was stabbed to death.

Settlement of the continent

In January 1788, a French expedition under the command of a captain called Jean François de la Pérouse arrived in Australia. De la Pérouse intended to claim the country for the French, but he was too late. Only the day before, the British had established a colony there.

On Easter Island in the South Pacific Ocean there are giant stone heads, some 12m (40ft) tall.

Locker room. Sails were stored here, carefully folded.

Boatswain's quarters. Ropes, tackle, pulleys and various other pieces of equipment were kept here.

Storerooms. Powder and ammunition for the guns.

33

Into the interior

Australia's coastline was well-mapped by the end of the 18th century. For many years, however, the interior remained a mystery to all except the local inhabitants, the Aborigines. There were many theories about what lay on the other side of the Blue Mountains. Some believed the land there was rich, and fertile, but others thought it was desert or marshland.

Robert Burke
(1820-61)

William Wills
(1834-61)

Besides the glory of being first to cross the continent, there was a need to set up a telegraph line to link Australia to the rest of the world. The men who first ventured into the interior suffered dreadful hardships and some even lost their lives. The journey of Robert Burke and William Wills best illustrates the bravery, misery, bad judgement and terrible luck experienced by so many of these explorers.

In 1859 the government of South Australia offered a prize to the first person to cross the continent from south to north. Burke and Wills were appointed leader and surveyor of one of the most expensively equipped expeditions in Australia's history. But there was one fatal flaw. Neither Burke nor Wills had any knowledge of the outback or much experience of exploration.

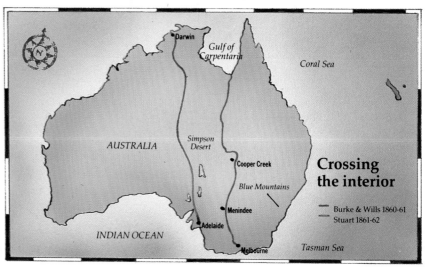

Crossing the interior

— Burke & Wills 1860-61
— Stuart 1861-62

The expedition sets out

The expedition left Melbourne in August 1860, cheered on its way by an enthusiastic crowd. Burke went first, followed by the other 15 members of his team and a long line consisting of 25 camels, 23 horses and wagons. After two months they had reached Menindee where they set up camp, but quarrels broke out among the men and Burke dismissed several of them. The expedition had now become very dispersed because of the varying speeds of parts of the team, with the wagons travelling long distances apart.

Hearing of a second, rival expedition, Burke became very impatient to move on. In scorching temperatures he, Wills and seven others set off for Cooper Creek, 645km (400 miles) northwest. The expedition was now divided into scattered groups. Once they arrived at Cooper Creek, Burke left one of the party, William Brahe, in charge of the remaining animals and provisions. Brahe was instructed to wait three months or until supplies ran out. Meanwhile Burke, Wills, Charles Gray and John King carried on to try and reach the Gulf of Carpentaria on the north coast.

Wildlife of the outback

The interior region of Australia is known as the outback. It contains many extraordinary plants and animals that are unknown elsewhere.

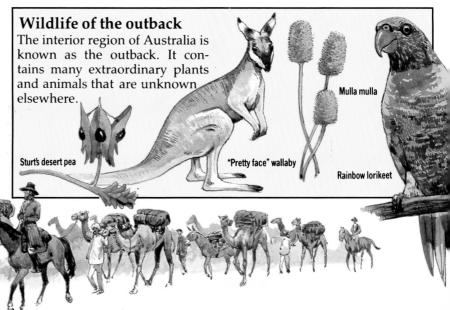

Sturt's desert pea

"Pretty face" wallaby

Mulla mulla

Rainbow lorikeet

Burke leading the expedition

Dead end

The weather suddenly changed and it rained endlessly for days. The ground became too waterlogged for the camels to move, so Burke and Wills went ahead on foot. By mid-February 1861 they were within sight of the shores of the gulf and could smell the sea. But their path was blocked by swamps of trees called mangroves and they decided to turn back.

The return journey

The journey south turned into a nightmare. Reunited with Gray and King, Burke and Wills headed back to Cooper Creek once more. Heavy rains fell for days on end, the men were soaked through to the skin and they became extremely feverish. The land turned into a quagmire of mud and slush. Food supplies were running so low that, one after another, the camels had to be shot for food and their baggage abandoned. Finally Gray, who seemed the strongest in the group, collapsed and died.

Aborigine

The deserted camp

Four days later, on 21 April, the three exhausted survivors staggered into Cooper Creek, hoping to find Brahe and the supplies waiting for them there. But instead they were horrified to find that the camp was deserted. They searched the place from top to bottom looking for supplies and eventually found a message left behind by Brahe. Believing they were dead, he had departed with the remaining animals for Menindee just seven hours before.

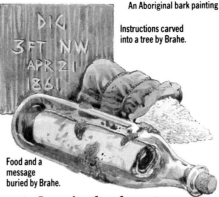

An Aboriginal bark painting

Instructions carved into a tree by Brahe.

Food and a message buried by Brahe.

Lost in the desert

Instead of trying to catch up with Brahe – unknown to them, he was only 23km (14 miles) away – Burke decided that they should return south by a shorter route towards Adelaide. They wandered in giant circles in the baking desert for weeks and ate the last of their camels. They were only saved from death because they were fed by some Aborigines who had been following them. The three exhausted men eventually found their way back to Cooper Creek.

To the Aborigines, the outback was a source of foods unknown to the explorers.

Witchetty grubs like this could be eaten raw.

The goanna (a type of lizard) could be captured and cooked.

By another incredible stroke of bad luck they had just missed Brahe once again. He had returned to Cooper Creek with a rescue party to look for them. But, seeing no sign that they had been anywhere near the camp, he moved on once more and headed back to Melbourne.

A tragic ending

Burke, Wills and King were only a few kilometres away, near to death. Their food had now completely run out and they began to slowly starve, growing weaker and weaker by the hour. King was the strongest and looked after the other two, doing as much as he could to help them. Wills was the first to die, followed by Burke some days later. King was now the only one left alive. Very weak himself, he staggered into the desert where he was looked after by some Aborigines living nearby. He was eventually found three months later by another search party from Melbourne. He was thin and burnt by the sun. Without the help of the Aborigines he would certainly have died. The remains of Burke and Wills were recovered and taken back to Melbourne for a state funeral.

Stuart wins the prize

Burke and Wills were the first to reach the north coast of Australia. But the first person to reach the coast and return alive was John McDouall Stuart. He was the leader of the rival expedition which left Adelaide in January 1861 in the race for the prize. This expedition arrived at the north coast seven months later. Burke, Wills and Stuart had proved that though much of the Australian interior was desert it was possible to travel across it.

John Stuart (1815-66)

Burke, close to death, is looked after by King.

The forbidden land

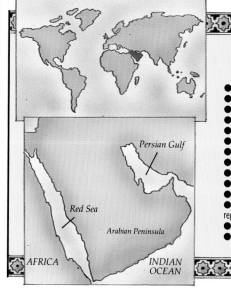

The Arabian Peninsula is surrounded on three sides by sea: the Persian Gulf, the Indian Ocean and the Red Sea. This made it a very important staging post on the trade routes from the Middle East, Africa, India and the Far East. Precious cargoes wound their way along the routes that criss-crossed the desert. Arabia also had valuable goods of its own to sell – incense, spices, drugs and perfumes, gold and precious stones. Because it was such a rich region, the Romans called it *Arabia Felix*, "Happy Arabia".

In contrast to the thin fertile strip along the south coast where rich kingdoms once flourished, further north the land rises steeply to a dry, barren region. Here nomadic tribes called Bedouin move flocks and herds between oases. In the centre of the peninsula are two fearsome deserts of shifting sand: to the north lies the Nefud while to the south lies the desolate Rub' al-Khali, the Empty Quarter.

A Bedouin encampment with tents made of goats' hair. ▼

An early adventurer

After the rise of Islam in the 7th century AD (see page 4), very few non-Muslims travelled in Arabia and the holy cities of Mecca and Medina were closed to all but Muslims. The first European to travel there after Covilhā's journey to Mecca in 1492 (see page 7) was a Venetian called Ludovico di Varthema. He arrived in Damascus in 1503 and set off disguised as a Muslim soldier in the pilgrim caravan to Mecca. He was the first non-Muslim to enter the Great Mosque and had many adventures before travelling on to India. He stayed there for some months before returning to Venice.

The rose-red city rediscovered

Johann Burckhardt was a Swiss scholar who had joined the Association for Promoting the Discovery of the Interior Parts of Africa (see page 8). He left for Africa via Syria, which he reached in 1809. He stayed in Aleppo for three years, learning Arabic and Islamic law.

The Khaznet Firaun (Pharaoh's Treasury) at the ▶ entrance into Petra.

On his way to Cairo in 1812, Burckhardt travelled through deserts and mountains to the remains of the fabulously rich city of Petra. This had been the capital of the merchant kingdom of the Nabataeans, who flourished from the 3rd to 1st centuries BC. Burckhardt was the first European to visit the city for over 1,500 years. He gazed on the Khaznet, a fantastic building carved from the pink-gold rock. Spellbound, he walked through the winding valley between elaborate tombs, temples and chapels, carved into the mountainsides and piled one above the other.

Johann Burckhardt (1784-1817)

Burckhardt reached Cairo and then travelled down the Nile Valley, stopping at the huge temple cut into the rock at Abu Simbel. He crossed the Red Sea to Jeddah and then visited Mecca, journeyed north through Arabia and arrived back in Cairo in 1815. Here he started to write up a report of his journeys. However, he died there two years later before he could continue his journey down into Africa.

El Haj Abdullah

In 1853 Richard Burton (see page 10) set sail from Suez in a pilgrim ship bound for Yenbo on the Red Sea coast. He went disguised as an Afghan doctor called El Haj Abdullah. The journey was chaotic, with fights breaking out among the pilgrims because of the lack of space. At the end of January they reached Medina where Burton stayed until August, writing an account of the city and its holy shrines.

Moving on, by the end of September he had arrived at the gates of Mecca. He prepared himself for entry into the city, shaving his head and donning the special white cotton pilgrim's robe. Inside the city, he took part in the holy ceremonies with hundreds of other pilgrims.

Burton had originally planned to cross the Arabian Peninsula from the west to the east coast. But, exhausted by the heat, he finally left Mecca at the end of the month and set sail for India.

Burton disguised as an Arab doctor.

A traveller's masterpiece

Charles Doughty (1843-1926)

Although Charles Doughty spent less than two years in just a small part of Arabia, he is now regarded as one of the greatest explorers of the region. During his travels he made no attempt to disguise the fact that he was a Christian European, even though it was still dangerous for non-Muslims to travel in Arabia.

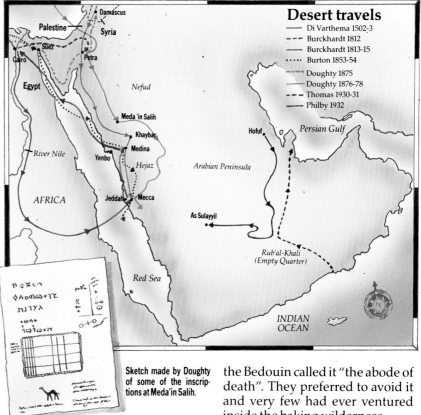

Desert travels
- Di Varthema 1502-3
- Burckhardt 1812
- Burckhardt 1813-15
- Burton 1853-54
- Doughty 1875
- Doughty 1876-78
- Thomas 1930-31
- Philby 1932

Sketch made by Doughty of some of the inscriptions at Meda'in Salih.

In 1875 he sailed to Palestine and by November 1876 he was in northern Arabia, studying the monuments at Meda'in Salih. Like those at Petra, they were cut into the mountains and decorated with ancient inscriptions. He travelled along the edges of the Nefud Desert with his Bedouin companions, making careful observations of their customs and the countryside they crossed.

At times Doughty was thrown out of towns because he was a Christian, but on other occasions he was warmly welcomed. In 1878 he returned to England and spent the following ten years writing one of the greatest works of travel literature, entitled *Travels in Arabia Deserta*.

Crossing the Empty Quarter

There remained one last little-known area of Arabia, the treacherous Rub' al-Khali Desert or Empty Quarter. This desert is so vast and forbidding that even the Bedouin called it "the abode of death". They preferred to avoid it and very few had ever ventured inside the baking wilderness.

This great sea of sand was finally conquered in the winter of 1930-31 when Bertram Thomas, an Englishman who was acting as adviser to the Sultan of Muscat, crossed the desert from south to north. The following year another Englishman called Harry St John Philby crossed the desert from east to west, travelling 3,000km (1,864 miles) over the burning sand in just 90 days.

Philby in Arabic dress.

Philby and his travelling companions in the Empty Quarter.

Around the world

People still sail round the world as a test of skill and endurance. But the first people to circumnavigate the globe had very practical reasons for their travels: trade and colonization.

Key dates in circumnavigation

- **Sept. 1519** Magellan leaves Spain.
- **Oct. 1520** Magellan travels through Straits of Magellan.
- **March 1521** Death of Magellan.
- **Sept. 1522** Remaining crew return to Spain.
- **Dec. 1577** Drake sets sail round the world.
- **Nov. 1580** Drake returns to England.

Western Europe and West Africa are shown twice on the map below. This is so that the routes around the world described on these pages can be shown clearly.

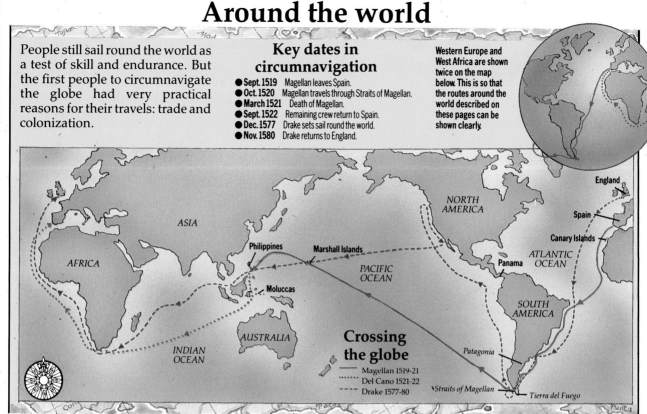

Crossing the globe

— Magellan 1519-21
···· Del Cano 1521-22
--- Drake 1577-80

Map labels: England, Spain, Canary Islands, NORTH AMERICA, ATLANTIC OCEAN, Panama, SOUTH AMERICA, Patagonia, Straits of Magellan, Tierra del Fuego, ASIA, AFRICA, Philippines, Marshall Islands, PACIFIC OCEAN, Moluccas, AUSTRALIA, INDIAN OCEAN

The first circumnavigation of the globe was led by a Portuguese aristocrat called Ferdinand Magellan. He had already made several journeys to find trade routes for the Portuguese, but he quarrelled with the king and went to sea for the Spanish instead. The Spanish wanted to establish trade routes to the East and claim territory there, particularly the Moluccas (Spice Islands). Magellan believed he could reach the Moluccas by sailing west round the southern tip of America, instead of following the Portuguese sea routes to the East around Africa (see page 18). Only two months after Magellan's arrival at the Spanish court, the young King Charles of Spain (later Emperor Charles V) agreed to finance the scheme.

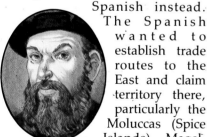

Ferdinand Magellan (c.1480-1521)

The fleet sets sail

In September 1519 Magellan left Spain with 260 men and five ships: the *Trinidad*, the *Vittoria*, the *Santiago*, the *Concepción*, and the *San Antonio*. They were carrying plenty of trading goods, but Magellan had underestimated the length of the voyage and did not take enough food and supplies. The fleet crossed the Atlantic, briefly stopping at the Canary Islands first. Then they sailed to Brazil and down the east coast of South America.

A mutiny and a shipwreck

Magellan encountered many problems. The weather was so bad that he decided to land for the winter on the coast of what is now

The Vittoria

Patagonia. Some of his men rebelled because of short rations and bitter cold, and he had to suppress the mutiny by executing the leaders. Later, the Santiago was shipwrecked.

The remaining ships finally found a route to the Pacific through a narrow sea passage now called the Straits of Magellan. From the ships, the crew saw fires that the natives had lit on the shore, so they named the area Tierra del Fuego ("land of fire"). Magellan's discovery of the straits named after him proved that there was another way to the East: to the south of the Americas.

Tierra del Fuego as it might have looked from the sea.

The starving sailors ate rats, animal hide and mouldy biscuits.

Disease, starvation, death

By this time conditions were worse. The *San Antonio's* crew deserted, sailing away with most of the fleet's food. Twenty men on the other ships starved to death as they crossed the Pacific.

After loading up with supplies at the Marshall Islands, the fleet continued to the Philippines. Here tragedy struck. Magellan became involved in a quarrel between local chiefs. He and 40 of his men were killed.

Magellan's successor

A captain called Sebastian del Cano took command of the 115 survivors. Without enough men to crew three ships, he abandoned the *Concepción*. The other ships sailed on, reached the Moluccas in November 1521, and bought the spices they set out for.

To improve the chance of getting at least some of the cargo home, the ships took two different routes back to Spain. The *Trinidad* went east towards the Spanish territory of Panama, but was seized by the Portuguese. Few of its crew survived.

A single ship returns

The *Vittoria* went westwards. It crossed Portuguese trade routes in the Indian Ocean and rounded the southern cape of Africa. It managed to avoid being captured, and reached Spain in 1522, having sailed round the globe in three years.

Francis Drake

The second great voyage of circumnavigation was led by an Englishman called Francis Drake. His voyage lasted from 1577 to 1580. At that time many people believed that Tierra del Fuego was part of a huge southern continent which they called Terra Australis. Others said the area was an island. Elizabeth I, the Queen of England, sent Drake to sail down the Straits of Magellan to find out which of these beliefs was true.

Francis Drake (c.1545-1596)

She also secretly expected him to bring back a good haul of treasure and spices. Both of them knew, however, that this would involve piracy and could damage relations between England and Spain. The expedition set sail in five ships: the *Pelican*, the *Marigold*, the *Elizabeth*, the *Swan* and the *Christopher*.

Drake plundered gold, silver, pearls and emeralds from Spanish ships.

Like Magellan, Drake suffered many hardships on his voyage. Storms, starvation and sickness provoked mutinies among his crew, but he pressed on through the straits. He did not find Terra Australis, but he did establish that Tierra del Fuego was an island. Drake returned to England on 3 November 1580. Queen Elizabeth visited him on board ship and knighted him.

Pigafetta's chronicle

Two pages from Antonio Pigafetta's account of Magellan's voyage.

This sand shark is probably the type Pigafetta saw.

One survivor of the voyage was an Italian sailor called Antonio Pigafetta. Most of our information about the journeys of Magellan and del Cano comes from his journal, which was published two years after his return. His account gives us many fascinating details of things he saw on his travels. These include man-eating sharks in the South Atlantic and a natural electrical phenomenon known as St Elmo's Fire. He recorded the terrible conditions the men endured, the cold and storms. He described the poor food and the stinking water they had to drink. He also wrote about the different people they encountered.

St Elmo's Fire made the ship's mast look as if it was burning.

The race for the Poles

Key dates in polar exploration

● **1893** Fridtjof Nansen leaves Oslo for the North Pole.
● **1908** Robert Peary and Mathew Henson set sail for the North Pole.

● **1909** Peary claims to have reached the North Pole.
● **1910** Roald Amundsen leaves for the South Pole.
● **December 1911** Amundsen and team reach the South Pole.
● **January 1912** Robert Scott and four others reach the South Pole.
● **February 1912** Scott and his companions die of cold.

The North Pole lies in the Arctic Ocean and the South Pole in the continent of Antarctica. They are the most hostile extremities of the Earth. By the end of the 19th century much of the world had been explored but the frozen polar wastes remained largely unknown. A number of determined explorers, however, set their sights on becoming the first to reach the Poles. It was a dangerous race and many people died in the attempt to win it.

The great Norwegian

One of the greatest of the Arctic explorers was a Norwegian called Fridtjof Nansen. For his journey to the North Pole, Nansen planned to use the drift of the ice in the Arctic Ocean to carry his ship along, rather than try and force a way through it. He designed a ship called the *Fram* ("Forward") that could withstand the pressure of the ice and drift with it until the spring thaw.

Fridtjof Nansen (1861-1930)

Nansen and his crew of 13 set sail for the North Pole from Oslo in June 1893. In September the *Fram* became locked into the

Arctic ice. From then on the boat had to go wherever it was carried.

The movement of the ice was terribly slow. They drifted for months, but instead of being drawn across the North Pole they began to move west. So Nansen and one other team member set off for the Pole with dogs, sledges and two kayaks (canoes). 386km (240 miles) from the Pole they turned back as the ice was beginning to break up with the onset of spring.

By pure luck they were later discovered by an English team on Franz Josef Land and travelled back with them by ship to Norway. The *Fram* arrived safely back with the others a week later.

Peary's claim

In 1886, Robert Peary of the United States Navy made the first of many expeditions to the Arctic. On this and five later journeys he travelled to Greenland, each time edging closer to the North Pole.

In July 1908 Peary and his assistant Mathew Henson set sail for their goal in the *Roosevelt*. At Etah in Greenland they recruited 50 Inuit (the local inhabitants) and gathered 250 dogs. In February 1909 the expedition moved off, with teams of Inuit setting up bases, and Peary, Henson and the dogs following.

Seals at the North Pole.

Peary and his team struggling over the ice and snow.

Gradually each team was sent back until only Peary, Henson and four Inuit, five sledges and 40 dogs were left. With the North Pole 214km (133 miles) away, this group set off on the final leg of the journey. It battled through blizzards, over ice ridges and perilous stretches of water.

On 5 April 1909 Peary recorded in his diary "The Pole at last!" believing he had finally reached his goal. However, experts raised doubts about whether he could have covered the distance so quickly. Despite recent attempts to prove that Peary did indeed reach the North Pole, the evidence remains questionable.

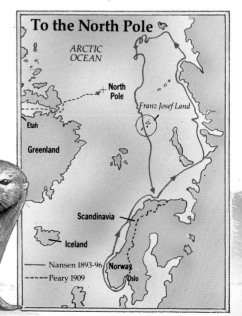

To the North Pole

ARCTIC OCEAN
North Pole
Franz Josef Land
Etah
Greenland
Scandinavia
Iceland
Norway
Oslo
—— Nansen 1893-96
----- Peary 1909

The *Fram* in the ice.

The triumph

In August 1910 a Norwegian explorer called Roald Amundsen set sail from Norway with eight others in Nansen's boat, the *Fram*. He originally planned to head for the North Pole, but hearing that Peary had reached it he decided to aim for the South Pole instead.

He was now entering a race against a British team that had already left for the South Pole led by Robert Scott, a captain in the Royal Navy. He sent Scott a telegram warning him that he now had competition.

Although he had to contend with the same appalling conditions as Scott did, Amundsen's expedition was much more efficient. It had fewer men so it could travel faster. Amundsen's men also wore lighter but warmer Inuit-style clothing.

They arrived at the Bay of Whales in January 1911 and set up camp at a point on the coast 97km (60 miles) nearer

Roald Amundsen dressed in his special Antarctic clothing.

the Pole than Scott's camp. They struggled through blizzards with their dog sledges, and reached the South Pole on 14 December 1911. After remaining there for three days they headed back to their base camp, which they reached on 25 January 1912.

Amundsen and his team were able to travel more quickly because they were using light, fast husky dogs rather than heavy horses.

The *Norge*

Later, in 1926, Amundsen became the first person to reach both Poles. He was a passenger on the airship *Norge* when it flew over the North Pole.

The tragedy

Two months before Amundsen, on 1 June 1910, Robert Scott set sail for the South Pole in the *Terra Nova* with a team of 53 men. The expedition was carefully planned and lavishly equipped, but the choice of equipment was to lead to a tragic ending: scientific machinery was to slow the team down; their clothes would prove inadequate against the bitter cold; horses were brought along to pull the sledges, rather than the lighter and faster husky dogs used by Amundsen, which were better suited to the terrible environment.

After a slow journey through the pack ice, their ship finally reached McMurdo Sound where they established their base camp.

Adélie penguins at the South Pole.

In January 1912 Scott set out on the last stretch with Lawrence Oates, Edward Wilson, Edgar Evans and Henry "Birdie" Bowers. The progress of this smaller team became slower and slower and eventually the horses had to be shot because they got stuck in the snow. The men now had to

The race south

South Pole

ANTARCTICA

Bay of Whales

McMurdo Sound

PACIFIC OCEAN

—— Scott 1910-12
----- Amundsen 1910-12

haul the sledges along themselves. On 18 January the exhausted team finally reached the South Pole, only to find the Norwegian flag flying there already.

Scott's team at the South Pole.

Disheartened, the men began the return journey to McMurdo Sound. But they were exhausted and frostbitten. With 692km (430 miles) to go, Evans collapsed and died. They eventually reached one of their depots, to find that the stored fuel oil had leaked away. There was now nothing to burn to keep them warm.

One night Oates, believing that he was holding up the team because he was so ill, walked out of their tent into the blizzard and was never seen again. His sacrifice was in vain for within two weeks the three remaining members were also dead. Their frozen bodies were found by a search party eight months later.

The roof of the world

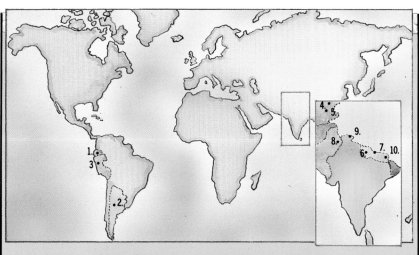

Key dates in mountain conquest

This chart lists ten of the world's highest mountains, in order of the date each one was first climbed. Each entry gives: the mountain's name and location; its height, the year of the expedition; the name and nationality of the expedition leader. The location of each peak is shown on the maps above.

1. Chimborazo, Ecuador; 6,267m (20,561ft). 1880, Whymper of Britain.
2. Aconcagua, Argentina; 6,960m (22,834ft). 1897, Zurbriggen of Switzerland.
3. Huascaran, Peru; 6,768m (22,205ft). 1908, Annie Peck of USA.
4. Lenin Peak, USSR; 7,134m (23,405ft). 1928, Soviet-German team led by Rickmers.
5. Communism Peak, USSR; 7,495m (24,590ft). 1933, Abalakov of USSR.
6. Annapurna, Nepal; 8,078m (26,504ft). 1950, French party led by Herzog.
7. Mount Everest, Nepal/Tibet; 8,848m (29,028ft). 1953, British party led by Hunt.
8. Nanga Parbat, Pakistan; 8,126m (26,660ft). 1953, Austro-German party led by Herrligkoffer.
9. K2 (Mount Godwin Austen), India; 8,611m (28,251ft). 1954, Desio, Lacedelli and Campagnoni of Italy.
10. Kangchenjunga, Nepal/Sikkim; 8,598m (28,208ft). 1955, Brown, Band, Streather and Hardie of Britain.

Since the very earliest times mountains have been regarded with awe and wonder. The peaks and summits were once believed to be the homes of gods and the cracks and crevasses the dwelling places of imps and demons. Howling winds echoed the eerie calls of the spirits and crashing avalanches warned people to keep away. Mountains such as Popocatepetl in Mexico and Mount Olympus in Greece have been worshipped as sacred places.

The earliest known climbs

For thousands of years people have feared mountains. It is only in the last 200 years that they have begun climbing them. Only a few genuine climbs are known to have been made in ancient times. In 350BC King Philip of Macedon climbed a mountain in the Balkans, and in about AD120 the Roman emperor Hadrian climbed Mount Etna to watch the sunrise.

Emperor Hadrian (AD76-138)

At the start of the Renaissance in Europe in the 14th century, people began to take a more scientific approach to their surroundings. Mountains were looked at in a different way, as places of interest rather than fear. The first known climb in the Alps took place on 26 April 1336 when the Italian poet Petrarch climbed Mont Ventoux (1,909m/6,263ft).

Petrarch (1304-74)

At first climbing was dangerous, for proper equipment was virtually non-existent. People simply wore warmer versions of everyday clothes. It was not possible to climb the highest peaks until suitable oxygen apparatus became available, because the higher a climber gets, the less oxygen there is in the air. This makes breathing very difficult. But as the years passed and experience increased, techniques were perfected and the equipment was improved. Mountaineers became able to climb higher and higher.

Modern mountaineering

Mountaineering as we know it today was developed by a Swiss scientist called Horace de Saussure. He was fascinated by the plants and rocks of the Alps, and in 1773 he made the first of many trips to the region. Gradually he became obsessed with the idea of climbing Mont Blanc, Europe's highest mountain at 4,807m (15,771ft), and offered a reward to the first person who could find a route to the top.

A plant from the Alps, Pygmy Ranunculus.

Early climbers caught in an avalanche.

The highest of all

No other mountain chain compares with the Himalayas. It contains the highest peaks in the world and stretches for thousands of miles across the length of northern India, and covers much of Sikkim, Nepal, Bhutan and southern Tibet.

In 1953 a British expedition led by John Hunt set off to climb Mount Everest, named after a British surveyor-general of India called Sir George Everest, but known locally as Chomolungma ("Mother Goddess of the World"). It is the world's highest mountain at 8,848m (29,028ft).

The climb to the final summit was made by the New Zealander Edmund Hillary and Tenzing Norgay of Nepal. On 29 May the weather cleared and they set off at 6:30am. On the way up their oxygen cylinders froze and there was a danger that they would not have enough oxygen. The going was extremely slow and they could only cover 0.3m (1ft) a minute.

The final obstacle was a sheer pinnacle of rock, 12m (40ft) high and covered with ice. Their route seemed to be blocked, but Hillary eventually found a way over it and edged himself up to the top. He then threw down a rope to Tenzing and at 11:30am on 29 May 1953, the two mountaineers stood alone at the top of the world.

The highest mountain in the world may have been conquered but many challenges still remain, including hundreds more peaks in the Himalayas and in other parts of the world. The urge to climb is as great as ever, spurred by the challenge, the thrill and glory of conquest and a deep respect for the mountains themselves.

Tenzing at the top of Everest

Many attempts were made but they were repeatedly driven back by avalanches, steep walls of ice and deep crevasses. One local doctor called Michel Paccard tried a number of times. On 7 August 1786 he set out once more, with a deer-hunter called Jacques Balmat acting as his guide. They reached the top of the lower slopes and spent the night there. The following morning they continued their hazardous journey up slippery

Michel Paccard
Jacques Balmat

peaks, over jagged edges and wading through waist-deep snow drifts; they finally reached the summit the same evening.

The following year, Saussure himself fulfilled his ambition by climbing to the top of Mont Blanc. 18 others went with him and they opened bottles of wine at the top to celebrate the achievement.

Saussure's climbing shoes

A climbing expedition in the late 18th century. Their clothing was unsuitable for the terrain and cold.

Hidden kingdoms of the Himalayas

After China broke off contacts with the West (see page 15) it once more became a land of mystery. But if China was remote, Tibet and Nepal, hidden away in the mountain fortress of the Himalayas, were even more inaccessible. In 1661 two Jesuit missionaries called John Grueber and Albert d'Orville became the first Europeans to reach Lhasa, the capital of Tibet. In 1811 a British official called Thomas Manning travelled in disguise to Lhasa, where he was received by the seven-year-old Dalai Lama (religious ruler) in the Potala Palace.

In the 1860s a French priest called Père (Father) David travelled extensively in Asia and China. He brought three animals to the attention of naturalists in the West: an unusual deer later named after him, a monkey named Roxellana's snub-nosed langur, and the giant panda.

Giant panda

Snub-nosed langur

Potala Palace, Lhasa

Père David's deer

Exploring the oceans

Key dates in undersea exploration

- **1690** Edmund Halley invents a method of pumping air down to diving machines.
- **1872** HMS *Challenger* starts its journey of exploration.
- **1930** William Beebe designs the bathysphere.
- **1943** Jacques Cousteau and Emile Gagnan design the aqualung.
- **1948** Auguste Piccard designs the bathyscape, *FNRS3*.
- **1950** *Challenger II* starts its journey of exploration.
- **1960** Jacques Piccard descends in the *Trieste*.

Nearly three quarters of the surface of the Earth is covered by water. For centuries people have been diving for precious underwater products such as pearls and natural sponges. But until the 20th century very little exploration had been made beneath the seas. This was because breathing apparatus was not available. Without it, divers could only stay below the water for as long as they could hold their breath.

Early diving devices

It is thought that in the 4th century BC Alexander the Great was lowered to the sea bed in a glass container to make observations. But he would probably have had to remain in shallow water because of the lack of air. It was not until 1690 that a method of pumping air down a pipe was invented, by an Englishman called Edmund Halley.

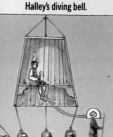

Halley's diving bell.

Going deeper

The deeper a diver goes in the sea, the greater the pressure of the water. In 1930 a North American called William Beebe designed the bathysphere, a spherical diving machine. Water exerts equal force all around a sphere, so it is able to withstand pressure at deep levels.

A modern bathysphere

Deep-sea red prawn
These types of fish are found at very deep levels.

In 1948 a Swiss scientist called Auguste Piccard designed a diving ship called a bathyscape. Known as *FNRS3*, it could dive and surface without having to be lowered and pulled up by a ship. On its first dive it reached a depth of 3,140m (10,300ft).

In 1960 Auguste's son Jacques Piccard descended nearly 11.25km (7 miles) in a craft called the *Trieste*. He reached the bottom

The *Trieste*

of the Mariana Trench in the Pacific Ocean. The journey down to the sea-floor took five hours.

Extra lungs

In 1943 two Frenchmen, Jacques Cousteau and Emile Gagnan, designed the first aqualung.

The aqualung consists of air cylinders containing compressed air and a mouth-piece. A "demand regulator" feeds the diver with exactly the amount of compressed air needed.

This invention opened a new period of underwater exploration and with its help many exciting discoveries have been made. Divers became able to descend to depths of 60m (200ft) without having to wear heavy protective suits and air cables. They were free to swim around and study underwater archaeology. They could photograph marine life, and also search for deposits of oil, tin, diamonds and other minerals.

Jacques Cousteau (1910-)

A diver using an underwater "scooter".

The *Challenger* expeditions

In December 1872 a British ship, HMS *Challenger*, set sail under the command of George Nares. There were many leading scientists on board, led by a Scottish naturalist called Charles Thomson, and many cabins were converted into laboratories. It covered a distance of nearly 112,650km (70,000 miles) across the Atlantic, Indian and Pacific oceans. Measurements down to the sea bed were made to determine its contours, and currents and weather conditions were measured. The ship returned to England in May 1876, full of facts and figures and 4,417 species of fish and underwater plants.

In 1950 the *Challenger II* set out across the Atlantic, Indian and Pacific oceans and the Mediterranean Sea. The latest echo-sounding equipment was used to make accurate recordings of the ocean floors.

HMS *Challenger* setting out on its journey of three-and-a-half years.

Angler fish

Sabre-toothed viper fish

Beyond the Earth

Key dates in space exploration

- **1903** Konstantin Tsiolkovsky publishes theory of rocket propulsion, recommending the use of liquid fuels.
- **1926** Robert Goddard launches first liquid-fuel rocket.
- **1957** *Sputnik I* launched by the USSR.
- **1961** Yuri Gagarin becomes first person in space.
- **1969** Neil Armstrong and Edwin Aldrin become first people on the Moon.
- **1971** *Salyut I*, the first space station, launched.
- **1977** Space Shuttle *Enterprise* makes first test flight.

Since the very earliest times the sun, the moon and the stars have always been objects of wonder and worship. Comets were believed to be warnings from the gods. Astronomy, the observation of the stars, is one of the oldest sciences. The ancient Egyptians were observing the planets thousands of years ago, and some people believe that Stonehenge in England, built in about 2500BC, was used as a giant observatory.

Early rockets

In order to travel in space, a rocket has to be powerful enough to break out of the pull of the Earth's gravity. In the 19th century a Russian scientist called Konstantin Tsiolkovsky made many experiments using liquid fuel. The first liquid-fuel rocket was launched in 1926 by an American called Robert Goddard. The flight lasted only 2.5 seconds but the break away from the Earth's atmosphere had been made. In October 1957 the Russians launched the first satellite into space, called *Sputnik I*.

Gird X, an early Russian rocket.

The first person in space

On 12 April 1961 a Russian astronaut called Yuri Gagarin became the first person to travel in space. His space-ship, *Vostok I*,

Vostok I

Yuri Gagarin (1934-68)

travelled at a speed of 8km (5 miles) a second, 160km (100 miles) above the Earth. Through his porthole, Gagarin

Telescopes

The first telescopes were invented in the 17th century. They enabled people to look at the moon and stars in more detail. The Italian scientist Galileo Galilei designed a stronger telescope. He was using it in 1610 when he discovered Jupiter's satellites, sunspots and mountains and craters on the Moon. Today, radio telescopes are used to detect radio waves coming from stars millions of light years away in space. These machines have discovered distant galaxies and strange objects like pulsating stars and black holes.

Galileo's telescope

The space telescope is designed to detect objects seven times further away than anything which can be seen from earth.

could see the world's surface laid out below him. *Vostok I* sped once round the Earth and after 108 minutes Gagarin returned, the cabin section of the spacecraft floating down on a parachute.

Exploring the moon

Tragically, Gagarin was killed in an air crash in 1968, before he could achieve his aim of being the first person on the moon. But his pioneering flights paved the way for Neil Armstrong and Edwin "Buzz" Aldrin of the United States to step out of their *Apollo* lunar module on to the surface of the moon on 21 July 1969. They took samples of rock and set up scientific equipment before returning to Earth.

One more manned lunar landing took place in 1969, two in 1971 and two in 1972. In 1970 and 1973 the Russians sent two unmanned vehicles called *lunokhods* to explore the surface of the moon.

The *Apollo 11* lunar module on the moon.

Space stations and probes

During the 1970s giant space stations, such as the Russian *Salyut* and American *Skylab*, were launched into space. They were laboratories orbiting round Earth and manned by crews who stayed aboard for a number of weeks on end without returning to Earth. One of the main purposes of these stations was to study the effect on people of long periods in space.

The US *Skylab* space station

Today space probes are sent to the more distant planets in the solar system. They carry cameras to take photographs and equipment to measure the temperature, magnetic fields and radiation of the planets. *Mariner 10* took about 4,300 close-up photographs of Mercury during three visits from 1974.

In the future

By the early 21st century people may be living in bases on the Moon. But we have only just started the exploration of space. So far unmanned spacecraft have landed on only two other planets in the solar system (Venus & Mars).

Key dates in world exploration

Dates BC

c.1492BC Queen Hatshepsut of Egypt sends out a trading expedition to the land of Punt.

c.600BC Pharaoh Necho II of Egypt sends out an expedition to explore the coasts of Africa.

c.450BC Herodotus draws a map of the world.

327-23BC Alexander the Great and his armies expand east from Persia.

c.300BC Building of the Great Wall of China begins.

138BC Chang Ch'ien leaves on a journey to Yuechi, China .

126BC Chang Ch'ien returns to China.

c.105BC Opening of the Silk Road, from China to the West.

Dates AD

AD150 Ptolemy draws his map of the world.

245 Chinese ambassadors travel to Funan (Cambodia).

304 Hsiung-nu (Huns) invade China.

629 Hsuan-tsang leaves China for India.

632 Death of the Prophet Mohammed, founder of Islam.

645 Hsuan-tsang returns to China.

c.860 Chinese reach Somali, Africa.
Vikings settle in Iceland.

c.900 Gunnbjorn sights Greenland.

c.986 Viking colony established on Greenland by Eric the Red. Bjarni Herjolfsson sights North America.

c.1000 Leif Ericsson lands on east coast of North America.

1002 Thorwald, brother of Leif, establishes a colony on the east coast.

1060 Chinese reach Malindi, Africa.

1162 Birth of Genghis Khan, later ruler of Mongols.

1187 Chinese reach Zanzibar and Madagascar, off the east coast of Africa.

1215 Genghis Khan captures Chung-tu (Beijing), capital of Chinese Chin empire, and establishes Mongol rule.

1240 Mongols capture Kiev, Russia.

1246 Giovanni da Pian del Carpini reaches the Mongol capital at Karakorum.

1253 William of Rubrouck sent to Karakorum.

1260 Kublai Khan proclaimed Great Khan.

1265 Niccolo and Maffeo Polo first reach the Chinese capital at Khanbalik (Beijing).

1269 Niccolo and Maffeo Polo return to Venice.

1271 Niccolo, Maffeo and Marco Polo leave Venice for China.

1292 The Polos leave China for home.

1325 Ibn Battuta travels to Arabia.

1368 The Mongols are driven out of China.

1394 Birth of Prince Henry of Portugal "the Navigator".

1405-33 Voyages of Cheng Ho in the Indian Ocean.

c.1420 The Chinese are believed to have rounded the Cape of Good Hope, Africa.

1434 Gil Eannes rounds Cape Bojador, West Africa.

1487 Bartolemeu Dias rounds the Cape of Good Hope. Pedro da Covilhã and Alfonso de Paiva set out from Portugal on their journeys East.

1492 Pedro da Covilhã visits Mecca.
Christopher Columbus leaves Spain for the East. He reaches and explores the "Indies".

1497 Vasco da Gama sails round Africa on his way to India.

1498 Da Gama visits Calicut.

1499 Da Gama returns to Portugal.

1503 Ludovico di Varthema visits Mecca.

1507 America is named after Amerigo Vespucci.

1511 Diego Velazquez and Hernándo Cortés sieze Cuba for Spain.

1519 Cortés sails to Mexico. Ferdinand Magellan begins his journey round the world.

1521 Siege of Tenochtitlán and fall of the Aztec empire.

1534 Jacques Cartier leaves France for North America.

1535 Cartier founds Montreal.

1569 Andres de Urdaneta crosses the Pacific.

1576 Martin Frobisher leaves England on his first voyage to find the Northwest Passage.

1577 Francis Drake sets sail round the world.

1585-87 John Davis makes three voyages to find the Northwest Passage.

1597 The Portuguese establish a trading station at Macao, China.

1606 Pedro Fernandes de Quiros reaches the New Hebrides Islands.
Willem Jantszoon becomes the first European to reach the shores of Australia.

1608 Samuel de Champlain founds Quebec.

1609 Henry Hudson sails along east coast of North America, in search of Northwest Passage.

1610 Hudson makes a second journey.

1642 Abel Tasman sights Van Diemen's Land (Tasmania). Tasman discovers the west coast of New Zealand.

1678-82 Robert de La Salle travels across North America.

1690 Edmund Halley invents a method of pumping air down to diving machines.

PACIFIC OCEAN   CARIBBEAN SEA   ATLANTIC OCEAN

1700 William Dampier, an English pirate, discovers the north coast of New Guinea.

1721 Jakob Roggeveen discovers Easter Island.

1769 James Cook sails in the *Endeavour* to Tahiti and makes observations of Venus. Sails on to New Zealand.

1770 Cook lands in Botany Bay, Australia.

1772 Cook's second voyage leaves Plymouth.

1774 Cook crosses the Antarctic Circle.

1776 Cook sets sail on his third voyage, in search of the Northwest Passage.

1779 Cook sails to the Sandwich Islands (Hawaiian Islands) where he is killed.

1785 François de la Pérouse leaves France in search of the Solomon Islands.

1788 De la Pérouse lands on the coast of New South Wales, Australia.

1795 Mungo Park sails to Africa.
Mathew Flinders and George Bass make the first inland expedition from the east coast of Australia.

1799 Alexander von Humboldt and Aimé Bonpland leave Europe for South America.

1801-2 Flinders carries out a survey of nearly all the coast of Australia.

1804 Meriwether Lewis and William Clark lead expedition across the United States.

1805 Park leaves on his second trip to Africa.

1810 Johann Burckhardt visits Palmyra, Syria.

1812 Burckhardt visits Petra, Palestine.

1813 Burckhardt rediscovers temple of Abu Simbel, Egypt.

1814 Burckhardt visits Mecca.

1817 Burckhardt dies in Cairo.

1824 René Caillié sets out from France for Timbuktu.

1828 Charles Sturt and Hamilton Hume cross the Blue Mountains, Australia.

1831 Charles Darwin leaves for South America in the *Beagle*.

1849 California Gold Rush.

1851 David Livingstone, his family and Cotton Oswell cross the Kalahari Desert, southern Africa.

1852-56 Livingstone becomes the first European to walk right across Africa.

1853 Richard Burton makes a pilgrimage to Mecca.

1856 Burton and John Speke leave England in search of the source of the Nile.

1858 Livingstone sets out to explore the Zambezi River.

1860 Robert Burke leads expedition from Melbourne to cross Australia from south to north.
Speke and James Grant leave on a second journey to Africa.

1861 John Stuart leads second, rival expedition to cross Australia, north from Adelaide. Death of Charles Gray, William Wills and Burke.

1862 Stuart returns south, having completed crossing of Australia.

1871 Henry Morton Stanley and Livingstone meet at the village of Ujiji, Africa.

1872 Livingstone starts out on his final African jouney, round the southern shores of Lake Tanganyika.
HMS *Challenger* starts out on its journey of exploration in the Atlantic, Pacific and Indian oceans.

1874 Stanley returns to Africa to map lakes Victoria and Tanganyika.

1875 Charles Doughty reaches Palestine.

1876 Doughty explores in the Nefud, northern Arabia.

1876-77 Stanley sails down the Lualaba and Congo rivers to the Atlantic.

1880 Edward Whymper climbs Mt Chimborazo, Ecuador.

1887 Stanley leads expedition to Sudan to find Emin Pasha.

1893 Fridtjof Nansen sets sail from Oslo for the North Pole.

1897 Mathias Zurbriggen climbs Mt Aconcagua, Argentina.

1908 Robert Peary and Matthew Henson sail for the North Pole. Annie Peck climbs to the top of Mt Huascaran, Peru.

1909 Peary claims to have reached the North Pole.

1910 Roald Amundsen and team leaves for the South Pole.

1911 Amundsen reaches the South Pole.

1912 Robert Scott and his team reach the South Pole.
Scott and team die of cold.

1916 T.E. Lawrence (Lawrence of Arabia) explores the Hejaz region in northern Arabia.

1925 Percy Fawcett disappears in the Brazilian jungle.

1926 Robert Goddard launches the first liquid-fuel rocket.

1930 William Beebe designs the bathysphere.

1930-31 Bertram Thomas crosses the Empty Quarter of Arabia.

1932 Harry Philby crosses the Empty Quarter.

1943 Jacques Cousteau and Emile Gagnan design the first aqualung.

1948 Auguste Piccard designs the bathyscape, *FNRS3*.

1950 *Challenger II* starts its journey of exploration.

1953 Edmund Hillary and Tenzing Norgay climb Mt Everest, Nepal/Tibet.

1957 *Sputnik I* launched by the USSR.

1960 Jacques Piccard descends to the bottom of the Pacific Ocean in the *Trieste*.

1961 Yuri Gagarin becomes the first person in space.

1969 Armstrong and Aldrin land on the Moon.

Index

The publishers are grateful to the following organizations for permission to reproduce their material, or to use it as artists' reference:

Bibliothèque nationale (Paris)

The Genesis Space Photo Library (Bideford, England)

The Mansell Collection (London)

Popperfoto (London)

First published in 1991 by Usborne Publishing Ltd,
83-85 Saffron Hill, London, EC1N 8RT, England.